Lost Eastwood
Edited by
Kiti Theobald

To my dear friend Doris
– enjoy!

Kiti Theobald

Lost Eastwood
Edited by Kiti Theobald

Copyright © 2012 Henry Smith

Published by
PB Software
3 Nelson Road
Ashingdon, Rochford
Essex SS4 3EJ

FIRST EDITION
First Printing June 2012

A CIP catalogue record of this book
is available from the British Library

ISBN 978-0-95659934-3-4

LOST EASTWOOD

A Glimpse of Eastwood's Past

CONTENTS

This book is a tribute to all those who participated in 'Project Eastwood'. Your time and effort have not been wasted. All the unused material will eventually be handed over to the Essex Record Office for safe keeping. Thanks to you all, the history of Eastwood has been recorded as well as possible for those who may seek out the village in years to come.

Also in thankful memoriam to those who have passed on before publication. We owe you all so much.

INTRODUCTION TO THE EASTWOOD BOOK

The Parish of Eastwood with its 1,000-year-old, Grade-One-Listed church of St Laurence and All Saints in Eastwoodbury Lane consisted of 3,300 acres; also in the past, it also encompassed Wallasea Island. It had 33 farms and 29 smallholding farms for ex-servicemen of the 1914-1918 War. Not one whole farm is now left due to the expansion and development of Southend.

Before 1933, Eastwood was part of Essex County Council. In 1933, it all became part of the Borough, with the exception of Blatches Farm, which was to be claimed by Hawkwell Parish, even though it stood south of the Roach Brook, the natural border between the two neighbouring authorities. The first farm to succumb to housing was Little Picketts Farm, south of Eastwood Road North, when Council houses were built on the farmland there.

Alarmed at the speed at which Southend Borough Council was eradicating the remains of Eastwood in its original situation, and how much St Laurence Church would be affected by developments at Southend Airport, a group of people got together to share and record their memories of Eastwood before it was all entirely forgotten, with the long-term plan to make it all into a book somehow.

The Group and its consequent display of findings went under the name of Project Eastwood, and the immensely successful display of artefacts and memories, both oral and visual, took place in the Church Hall, attracting large numbers of people who wanted to know about the history of the Parish.

Of course, after the Exhibition, everything was put away, and the task of assembling it into a more manageable size was begun. This turned out to be much harder than we had envisaged, but finally has been achieved.

There will always be those who feel that any change is progress, and as many others who question the amount of change that has to happen; either way, Eastwood has changed beyond all recognition. The grid that forms part of the Southend coat of arms is that of St Laurence, and the church that bears his name is a thousand years old. The Saxon/Norman church of St Mary's, Prittlewell, and the Benedictine Priory are of similar antiquity and Southend itself merely the 'south end' of Prittlewell, being originally a cluster of fishermen's cottages. And yet it is Southend which has grown and incorporated all the surrounding settlements into one unitary authority, almost too large for its own stability.

This is not a book written by professionals, but by a group of enthusiastic amateurs, who wanted you to share their love for a part of Southend which has almost disappeared.

Our thanks go to all who contributed information to the book, a number of whom have written a little memoir of their lives for Chapter 3, but especial thanks to Grace Panton for setting the ball rolling and organising 'Project Eastwood', to Henry Smith, for his patient reassembly of the information into manageable pieces, to Sid Broomfield for his accurate recall of Eastwood and the changes it has undergone and not least to Derek Theobald for his patient and accurate proofreading.

And thanks to you, dear Reader. Memory Lane is a lovely place to be, so journey with us into:

'LOST EASTWOOD'.

Project Eastwood attracted hordes of visitors to the St Laurence Church Hall

St Laurence & All Saints Eastwood

☩   ## ROLL OF HONOUR   ☩

1914
		### 1918
L Aldridge	G W Bacon	H Bacon
A L Bowring	C W Cox	S E Edwards
W A Easlea	S R Grant	W Havis
A Hoare	J Hoare	C J W Jones
S Lamb	A G Lay	H G Layzell
A J Maynard	W McLellan	C Moss
B Nunn	H J Nunn	F N Powling
C H Rice	W Shuttleworth	A G Taylor
W R Taylor	A E Turner	T Webb
	A S Wells	

1939
		### 1945
T J G Davies	R A W Davison	J Katlofer
D L Leonard	E C Martin	E Moore Tabb
A L Nichols	G A Spalding	P G Spicer
W P Taylor	W T Taylor	E B Turpin

1951   L Millikin

They shall grow not old, as we that are left grow old:

At the going down of the sun, and in the morning

We will remember Them

CHAPTER ONE
EASTWOOD WITHIN LIVING MEMORY

The memories of some of our contributors have gone back to the early 20th Century, and with their help we have been able to create a picture of life as it was during that time. We have been able to name the brickfields, the farms, the characters who populated the village, as it was then, the trades and professions, the schools and basic geography of Eastwood.

The main occupation of the first 50 years of 20th-Century Eastwood was anything allied to farming, since much of Eastwood was reputed to have the most fertile soil, known as Grade 1,2 and 3 agricultural land, although the village was not exclusively agricultural. It would seem that Eastwood was self-sufficient in so many ways before being swallowed up by Southend, with its own farms, smallholdings, garage, smithy, shop and deliveries and so on.

Cattle from Eastwood Farms were sold at Rochford Market
This was Christmas 1928

Farming has therefore been given its own chapter in the order of things, and the whole picture will be given added colour by calling on some of the characters themselves, along with first-hand accounts of life in Eastwood.

There were at least 8 brickfields within the parish of Eastwood, along with over 30 farms. It does not sound as if there would be enough room within this small settlement to contain all this, but it has to be said that the original Parish of Eastwood was much greater in former times then it is now, encompassing land from The Horse and Groom public house in Rochford, the eastern boundary being Sutton Ford Bridge; Rochford Hall itself, the whole of Green Lane to the Rayleigh Boundary, which was further west than it is today, taking in Eastwood Lodge, The Woodcutters public house, Coombes Corner and westwards to The Priory Farm where Priory Crescent runs today.

The brickfields were

- Cornish's, in Rayleigh Road opposite Dandies Drive

- Gale's, on the left of Lambeth Road/Hudson Road

- Cherry Orchard, in Cherry Orchard Lane

- Powlings/ Wagstaffs at the bottom of Eastwood Rise

- Leighfields, in Bellhouse Lane

- Charlie Benson's, now the site of St David's

- Featherby's, by the Horse and Groom, Rochford

Brickfield soil was light, fine clay, ideal for brick making. Bricks would be left in racks out in the sun to dry them before they went into the kilns. Each brickyard had its own kilns to 'fire' the bricks. In the Wagstaff brickyard, below Hillside Road, there were 5 kilns for making the bricks. After the land was turned over to farming, the scorch marks in the soil could be seen every time the land was ploughed, for years afterwards. This brickyard was run by Mr Wagstaff, but owned by Mr Powling, who later moved to the Trout Fisheries at Stambridge. Mr Powling had once been sued over obstructing the right-of-way to Flemmings Farm by Mr Sparrow, one of the family of vets who cared for all the livestock and pets in the area.

Mr Clark, Number 8 Small Holdings

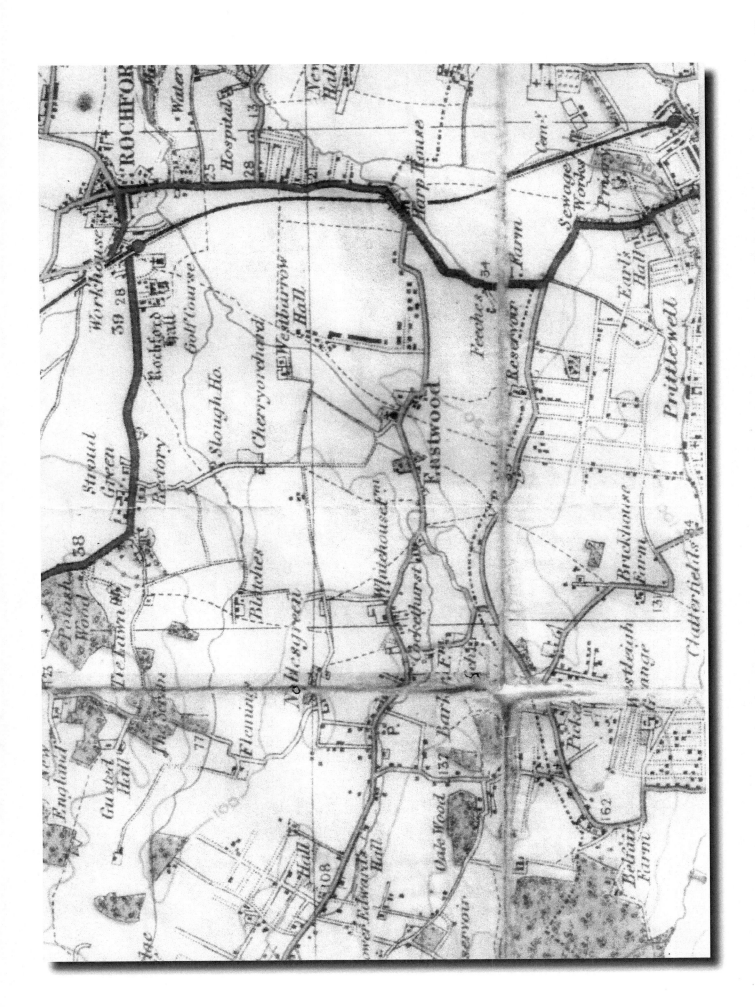

3

There were 29 Smallholdings in the village, and several nurseries, as well as the farms. Mr Clark lived at No 8, Smallholdings. Sid and Alf Stokes were brothers who each kept nurseries; Sid farmed off the A127, west of the Airbourne factory, and Alf's smallholding ran from the edge of the Progress Road Estate to Thompson's bungalow on the Rayleigh Road. The produce from the nurseries was taken to Covent Garden.

Some of the nurseries are remembered by the name of the nursery, and others by the name of the owners and growers. The Smith Family grew tomatoes, flowers and seedling plants, and Mullocks sold tomatoes and mushrooms in Rayleigh Avenue. Other nurseries were at Noraville (now a house along the Rayleigh Road), Appledene, The White House (owned by Councillor Court), and Broadclyst Nursery, owned by the Warrens. This stood next to Lower Edwards Hall Farm land, and is now occupied by a Tesco and several DIY units towards Progress Road. Munn's nursery gave its name to Munn's Corner, which later became Rochford Corner.

An artist's impression of Munn's Corner

Sonny Jolly was at the top of Eastwood Rise, along with Scraggs, who rented Edwards Hall for a time about 1914, just before World War One. Clarke's Nursery also housed pigs in his smallholding, and next door to him was Mr Keoch, head of a German family, also owners of a nursery. Doe had his own nursery as well as working for Mr Fowler, who sold retail vegetables.

Mr Stone kept an orchard on the A127, where there were also smallholdings owned by Fox, Bagnall and Spray. Mr Bull lived opposite Southbourne Grove in the last smallholding.

There was also Boosey's nursery, just beyond Tinkers Lane, though still within the Eastwood boundary. Jackaman's had two, later three smallholdings at Big West Farm as well as owning farm land. These nurseries were either side of bridle path 10.

Mr Bridges (of whom more later in Chapter Three), took his horse and cart all around the area, loaded with fruit and vegetables to all the inhabitants of Eastwood.

From an exhibition at Rayleigh in 2000

Airborne Industries

Walkers Butchers took over the old Post Office and Telephone Exchange, the Post Office moved to Weston Stores in the early 1930's on the corner of Dandies Drive

Congregational Church

Eastwood Mission Hall

EASTWOOD CONGREGATIONAL HALL.

DEDICATION & OPENING.

DEAR FRIEND,

We have the greatest possible pleasure in inviting you to the SERIES OF MEETINGS in connection with the above on WEDNESDAY, DECEMBER 14th, 1927:—

SERVICE at 4 p.m.;

TEA at 5.30 p.m.;

PUBLIC RALLY at 7 p.m.

The Church Extension Committee of the Essex Congregational Union generously purchased a site for this purpose nearly a year ago.

Fencing, laying out the ground, erection and furnishing the Hall, which was a disused Schoolroom, has cost a little over £150.

We feel that this is not an amount beyond the power of united Congregationalism to raise immediately, so that so young a cause may not be hampered with debt.

May we ask for your very kind and generous assistance.

Yours very faithfully in Christ's Service.

W. BUCKLEY, *Hon. Sec.*,
Tudor Road, Eastwood;
C STONE, *Hon. Treas.*
"Morning Dawn," Eastwood.

Mr Bridges was only one of a number of hauliers in the village. Obviously, in an area with so much farming and brick making, hauliers were an important part of the process and aided the local economy. The Beckwith's, three generations of them, worked out of a house which they had built themselves in Eastwood Rise, known as Rose Marie. They started business with one lorry, and moved on when Sid, Ken and John Beckwith took over and enlarged the business. They ended up as general hauliers, hauling bricks and anything else they were asked to move!

Garland's stood on the Rayleigh Road, near to where the Police station stands today. Their business began from one of the wooden cottages that used to stand opposite the Memorial Hall.

Mr Pickering, who operated from a site north of the Rayleigh Road entrance to Eastwood Park, picked up the churns of milk from all the farms with his lorry for the Co-op Dairy. Mr Quinnell, who also kept pigs in Nore Road, off Eastwood Rise, was a local coalman. His depot was in Eastwood Old Road. This was a thriving business in those days, as everyone had coal fires to heat their houses and their water supply.

The Smiths operated Stanway Contracts, Ltd, which mostly used tipper lorries; other tippers were operated by Brush, who lived in Gravel Road. The local builder was called Ardleigh. We cannot leave this section without also mentioning the knitting factory and Ecko factories, the Post Office at Eastwood and Airborne Industries which were all within Eastwood boundaries, providing opportunities for work other than agriculture, thriving alongside the farms, smallholdings and brickyards in this 3000-acre Parish.

There were two doctors in Eastwood, but if these were unavailable, it would be necessary to go to Rochford for medical help. There were two or three midwives and the chemist, Mr Joy, who was said to be as good as a doctor when dealing with most complaints. Nurse Powell, the Rochford Midwife, was buried in St Laurence churchyard, and Granny Gooch, who lived at the end of Brickfield Cottages in Hillside Road, was the one called upon by the itinerant gypsy population when a baby was due to be born. Hans and Sheila Fleming were doctors at Rochford Corner in the mid-nineteen-forties before moving to Kent Elms, and another doctor was remembered as Dr Fiddis. He saved Mrs Broomfield's life in 1933, when her pregnancy resulted in a breech birth, and he never charged for his services.

There were and always have been a number of travellers in Eastwood, the names of Bibby, Buckley, Stone, Hedges and Spearman being the most prolific. The travellers were accomplished in farm work, from potato lifting and planting to fruit picking, and they worked alongside the women and children from the village. Mrs Dale, who lived in Eastwood Rise at 'The Rest' was the ganger for the potato people; she could pick up 45cwt (hundredweight) of potatoes in one day, setting an almost impossible target for the rest of the lifters! She would also settle the price for the job with the farmer concerned.

The travellers did not rely solely on their farm work, but also made artificial flowers and baskets from willow, or pegs which could be whittled from wood and sold door-to-door.

Before leaving this chapter, we must return to the ancient centre of the village, which of course, has to be St Laurence Church. There is a whole chapter dedicated to the church, which is the oldest in the area, but since Eastwood's population has increased, so has the number of churches which serve the population. St David's and St Aidan's, St Peter's and St Stephens are all offshoots of St Laurence. The Baptist and Congregational churches have also grown up within the parish of Eastwood, as well as the Catholic church of St Margaret's on the corner of Hillside Road, and St Cedd's in Bridgwater Drive.

CHAPTER TWO
ST LAURENCE CHURCH

General View from a south easterly direction - Spring 2004

'The Wonderful Door'

EASTWOOD. Here the lover of smith-craft will rejoice, for the ancient ironwork still gives strength to doors which have opened and closed for 20 generations.

Close-up of Saxon ironwork on the south door

Southend is swallowing up Eastwood, but toward the Church still linger charming cottages built of wood and roofed with thatch. On Rochford Way stands the Old Workhouse, with an upper storey projecting and a wing built in the days when Joan of Arc was driving our army out of France.

In front of a row of elms a border of grass creeps up to the churchyard wall, and two sycamores stand before a 16th Century porch made beautiful with carved bargeboards on its gable. The roof of the church

The old workhouse, Southend Road circa 1750

has a high pitch reaching up beside the wooden tower and covering both nave and aisle in its downward sweep. The tower has stood 700 years, supporting a slender spire, and is itself borne on a stone tower attached for some strange reason to the (south) aisle. The door in the brick porch is one of the most wonderful doors in Essex. For six-and-a-half centuries it has swung on these hinges, the planks held firm by scrolls and flowers hammered out of iron, yet when the smiths fashioned this piece of beauty they used once more the strap-hinges their grandparents had wrought for a still-earlier door, with its boldly cut prayer of peace for those who come this way, and those who go. A door inside the church, equally beautiful, has been the companion of this all down the ages, and used to hang in the doorway now blocked up in the opposite aisle. There is ironwork on both doors, making them precious possessions for a village.

Close by is a masterpiece in stone, a Norman font with interlacing round arches encircling a tapering bowl. Norman arches older than the font are high up on the walls of the nave, one complete, the others only in part. In this aisle is a curious partition of oak, placed here in the 15th Century to give the priest a private room. In the aisle is the trapdoor through which the priest used to climb up; it is stiff on its old hinges.

The door to the priest's room

The chancel has a brass portrait of Thomas Burrough, who died three years before Elizabeth, and the wooden tower has two bells which have called the village to worship for over 500 years.'

Editor's note – Arthur Mee might be mistaken about this figure as the door and its strapwork date from the Norman period.

Arthur Mee wrote this in 1940 in a book entitles "The King's England – Essex. Today the southern aspect of the church is not as picturesque as it was in 1940; the 'row of elms' so eloquently described has all gone, thanks to the ravages of the Dutch Elm beetle; also the encroaching airport, with its plans for expansion, seems to want to take a little more of the flora from the south and east side.

Thomas Burroughs' memorial brass

The smallholdings directly opposite the church have also gone, to make way for the runway extension, but as isolated as the church may appear today, its role as the centre of a thriving community is still very vital, and it is a treasured building.

Church cottages from the churchyard

In the church floor, by one of the supporting columns of the arcade, is an ancient boulder, which could have been here since the Ice Age. It protrudes above the otherwise level floor of the chancel, and is a feature found in many old churches of similar antiquity. It is thought that this could have marked the meeting place of the villagers of Eastwood before the building of the first church on the site. It is a fact that the Saxons bringing Christianity to England would often utilise the existing places of worship to assemble and to disseminate the new religion to the pagans already there.

The list of incumbents, which had been painted on one of the columns of the arcade, has been modernised on to a wooden tablet, and clearly predates AD 1250, when the first member of the clergy was recorded. Some of the names have been investigated and some interesting histories have been discovered. For instance, William de Rothwell, who was parson in Eastwood for only four years in the 14th Century, became concerned that tithes from Rayleigh Park had been paid in error to the parson of Rayleigh, when they should have come to Eastwood. This obviously amounted to a sum that was impossible to ignore, as William was obliged to petition the King, Edward III, in order to obtain redress.

William's audacity must have brought him to the notice of someone in authority, as he was soon given the post of Minister of War. In 1340, Edward had declared himself King of France, thereby initiating The Hundred Years' War. William de Rothwell's role in this war was to keep the soldier's supplied with weapons. In 1358, he was ordered to deliver 500 bows, 200 painted and 300 'white', along with 100 sheaves of arrows for service in Brittany. A year later, he was ordered to cause all bows, arrows, bowstrings and crossbow winches to be sent to Sandwich for the King's passage overseas. Edward and his son, the Black Prince, had routed the French at Crecy in 1346.

*The lych gate designed and erected by Ron Emmett, the choirmaster in the mid-1980's
and built by Mr Arthur Collins and Southend Technical College students*

Before his death in 1361, William de Rothwell held many prestigious posts. In 1353, he became Warden of The Tower of London, and keeper of the King's wardrobe. At this time, the arsenal ready for fighting the French consisted mainly of arrowheads. By 1360, he had raised this to 15,365 bows, 4,000 bow staves, 567,432 arrows, and 22 breastplates, but this and more was needed for the next expedition, so he must have worked hard to maintain this amount of weapons and ammunition.

William is also recorded as being the prebendary of Chichester, Lincoln and Salisbury cathedrals, as well as for The Chapel Royal at Westminster, so he would have been very close to the King himself. His tomb in Holy Trinity church, Rothwell, Northamptonshire, states that he was also archdeacon of Essex, all these titles no doubt having been granted by the king by way of reward for his services in times of war. He must at any rate have been an extremely well-educated man, well able to handle several different tasks at an extremely high level. The brass on his tomb shows him wearing a long robe with buttoned sleeves. Around his neck is a type of fur hood, with a fur stole hanging in front. The translation of the inscription reads as follows:

"NOW, CHRIST, 1 PRAY THEE HAVE MERCY, 1 ENTREAT, THOU WHO CAMEST TO REEDEEM THE LOST, CONDEMN NOT ME, WHOM THOU HAS REDEEMED, FOR THE SOUL OF WILLIAM DE ROTHWELL, WHO IS HERE BURIED, ARCHDEACON OF ESSEX, PREBENDARY OF CROPRYTY, FERRYING AND YALMETON AVONS, PRAY TO THE KING OF GLORY TO HAVE PITY ON HIM, IN HONOUR OF HIM SAY DEVOUTLY A PATER NOSTER AND AN AVE"

The de Rothwell memorial

In the 17th Century, brothers Samuel and Thomas Purchas held the living for 48 years between them. During Thomas's stewardship, a man of Eastwood was fined 'for sleeping in the time of divine service upon a Sunday afternoon this last summer, and so sat sleeping until all the people were gone forth from the church'!

In the 18th Century, the legendary actor, David Garrick came to hear George Morrison preach a burial service, as George was renowned for being a fine, impressive reader.

It would be interesting to research the other 65 known incumbents to find out if any of them have interesting anecdotes or stories to tell us.

The list of incumbents is as follows:-

GEOFFREY	1250	JOHN FLAXMAN	1554
RICHARD	1261	ROBERT HART	1562
RICHARD de	1274	CHRISTOPHER KITCHEN	1571
WILLIAMWYGEYN	1303	HENRY SLEDD	1592
ROGER de SPYNETO	1313	SAMUEL PURCHAS	1604
WILLIAM de HERLASTON	1315	THOMAS PURCHAS	1614
WILLIAM de ROTHWELLE	1325	PHILOGUS SACHEVERELL	1652
JOHN de WYSETTE	1328	ROBERT POOL	1662
JOHN de FARNISHAM	1338	ROBERT SMITH	1666
JOHN HOLBECKE		WILLIAM KNIGHT	1668
JOHN de HONESDON	1362	RAYMONDUS GACHEUNS	1673
GILES de WYNGREMONTH	1376	FRANT BARBAT	1684
THOMAS OCLE	1380	PETER PERES	1697
JOHN MALLORY	1384	GEORGE MORRISON	1748
WILLIAM FESANNT	1386	FRANCES FORDYCE	1763
JOHN HOLBECK	1393	JOHN BLAKE	1766
THOMAS CALSWELL	1393	RICHARD STUBBS	1781
THOMAS	1417	RICHARD MITCHELL	1810
RICHARD GREGONIC	1453	GEORGE PRICE	1826
WILLIAM TOLLETT	1459	WILLIAM C RAY	1857
JOHN MALPAS	1465	EDWARD M BIRCH	1866
ROBERT EDMUNDS	1477	JOHN SPENCER	1867
WILLIAM EVERSHAM	1481	GEORGE V PROCTOR	1900
LAURENCE ASHRON	1486	JOHN W CASSELLS	1904
WILLIAM THETCHER	1504	HUGH HORSLEY	1906
RICHARD THORNTON	1505	ARTHUR SYKES	1912
RICHARD WILTCHER	1509	FRANK E CROWTHER	1916
THOMAS ELLIS	1512	HENRY D RICE	1930
WILLIAM LAKENHAM	1520	HENRY J COBBETT	1936
RAYMOND MOLINAX	1521	ROBERT C A BYRNE	1948
THOMAS STONE	1524	HERBERT D WOOLCOTT	1956
ROBERT MERY	1531	MICHAEL BALLARD	1978
WILLIAM ANTON	1540	NIGEL L RANSOM	1991
RICHARD PARKINS	1552	STEPHEN SPENCER	2011

Churchyard

Lammas Tide 1933 with Revd Byrne

EASTWOOD CHURCH GARDEN FÊTE

AND

Horticultural Society's Show,

WEDNESDAY, JULY 13th, 1910,

IN THE

Vicarage Grounds, Eastwood.

Opening Ceremony at 3.15 p.m., by Mrs. JAMES TABOR.

All the usual ATTRACTIONS, including:

High-class Concerts, Waxworks, Aunt Sally, Cocoanut Shies, Hoop La, Shooting Gallery, Quoits, Swings, Greasy Pole, Bicycle Gymkhana, Competitions, &c.

☛ *MILITARY BAND.*

Do not miss the **HORTICULTURAL SOCIETY'S SHOW** (2nd Annual), also the Exhibition of **BEE-KEEPING APPLIANCES.**

All SIDE SHOWS, except the Bicycle Gymkhana, will be held in the field, and are **absolutely FREE.**

Note the Date: **WEDNESDAY, July 13th, 1910.**

ADMISSION : 3 to 6 p.m., **6d.** ; after 6 p.m., **3d.**

For further particulars apply to GEO. W. NEWLAND, Hon. Sec., Fête Committee.

Send all Entries for Show to R. MacCOLLA, Hon. Sec., Horticultural Society.

Those who use the church are justifiably proud of its fine tower and spire. The shingles on the spire were replaced in 1957 and again in 2008, the latter occasion due to woodpeckers nesting within the spire. The former shingles were made of cedar wood, but the current shingles are made of oak, which are supposed to deter woodpeckers!

The outside of the church has obviously changed a great deal through the Centuries. The first church building could have been built of wood or stone, but by the early 17th Century the church was in a ruinous state. When the old exterior plastering was stripped off, part of the building showed the original rubble with red Tudor brickwork on top, three to four feet in depth and above the windows. Where some corners had given way they too were replaced by Tudor brick and reinforced by a brick buttress.

The front boundary of the Churchyard of Eastwood St Laurence is a brick wall with a wood and iron double gate through which entrance is obtained. A stone stile is situated on the right hand side of the entrance, over which brides are traditionally carried by their grooms.

The 'Steps in the wall' next to the south gate. These were used in the days of the horse and carriage to aid mounting and alighting

The entrance proper to Saint Laurence and All Saints is through the 16th Century Porch which is made of red brick. The niche over the doorway, together with the partly filled-in Holy Water container would imply that the building was finished before The Reformation. Wooden benches are situated along both sides, together with small windows; it is likely that this area was used as a school for the local children.

An interesting feature of the south door is the triangular knocker generally regarded as a Sanctuary Knocker, for this was a time when the church could offer sanctuary to those who had done wrong and flung themselves upon the mercy of God. There is an incident recorded in the rolls of King Edward I, who was hunting in this district, that a man was pardoned at the insistence of Lady Eleanor De Percy, after being condemned to be hanged for stealing three pigs. The rope broke and he escaped, fleeing to the church for sanctuary. He was later exiled.

The north door is used as the entrance to the choir vestry which was completed in 1966; it is as beautifully decorated with strapwork as the south door.

The float Friends of St Laurence entered in the Southend Carnival in 2003 Model made by Mr. W. Robinson.

The tower below the beautiful spire houses 6 bells now. Two date from the 14th Century and one from the 17th. In 1984 the tower was strengthened to hold a new metal bell frame and the three old bells were re-hung and augmented to a ring of six by the addition of three lighter bells. During this work, one of the old bells (now the 5th) which was cracked was repaired by welding. The iinscriptions on the bells are as follows:-

Tenor	9cwt 8lbs	Sancta Gregori ora pro nobis (StGregory pray for us) (cast 1380)
5	6cwt 6lbs	Sancta Katerina ora pro nobis (St.Katherine pray for us) (cast 1380)
4	4cwt 2qtr 2 lbs	Charles Newman made me 1693
3	4cwt 12lbs	We praise thee O God in memory of Ethel and Gladys Fowler of Cockethurst Farm
2	3cwt 1 qtr 8lbs	O come let us sing unto the Lord in memory of Ranie & May Fowler of Cockethurst Farm
Treble	2cwt 3qtr 16lbs	Unto thee O Lord do we give thanks the gift of Mabel Free

Peter Knight rehangs one of the bells - 1986

The tower is only two metres square and is thought to be placed in an unusual position at the west end of the south aisle. The lowest stage of this is early 13th Century, so it is not some modern idea, but part of the first stone church on the site.

The South Aisle Altar Window

There are two aisles, north and south, but whereas the south aisle is more or less as you would expect, it is the north aisle that is the more unusual It is 14th Century, and after all this time, is difficult to say why this narrow addition was made. In the East wall is a 14th Century Late Decorated window with two cinquefoil windows - partly restored. At the west end of the aisle is an unusual feature, a priests' room, an oak framed apartment of two stages lighted by a small 15th Century square headed window. The chamber contains an oak bier, dated 1706 and the screen is 15th Century oaken work with moulded and embattled head and rail. It is thought that it could have been used as overnight accommodation by the monks who came from the Cluniac Priory at Prittlewell. The lower chamber is now used as the Vicar's Vestry. In the reign of Henry II the church was a chapel to Prittlewell Priory and the monks were sent to conduct services at St Laurence church.

One of the most modern features of the church and also one of the most beautiful must be the west window. The original frame is 15th Century, with modern stained glass depicting the life of Samuel Purchas, the geographer, writer and Vicar of Eastwood between 1604 and 1614. It was in 1978, through the generosity of Miss Gladys and Miss Ethel Fowler that the new window was completed and dedicated. It incorporated events and places within the Parish of Eastwood.

It was in 1604, that Samuel, a graduate of Saint John's College, Cambridge and son of George Purchas, a yeoman of Thaxted, Essex was inducted as Vicar of Saint Laurence and All Saints. He remained here for ten years, during which time his interest turned to the study and research of the history of exploration. This was probably due to conversations with local seafarers and to John Vassal, who was living at Cockethurst Farm and was a member of The Virginia Company of London.

The West Window

In 1598 a geographer and author Richard Hakluyt, who was Prebendary of Bristol and Westminster Abbey published a work entitled "The principal Navigational Voyages, Traffiques and Discoveries of the English Nation." with a description of the country, commodities, people, government and religion.

While he was at Eastwood, Samuel Purchas started his own monumental work on exploration which was dedicated to George Abbot, Archbishop of Canterbury. In 1614, Samuel was appointed as Rector of Saint Martins, Ludgate Hill, by the then Bishop of London, John King and left Eastwood.

Starting at the top of the window there are six small sections, the two lion masks at the centre are from Cockethurst Farm, flanked by two anchors and the initials J and L for Jane Lease, the maiden name of Samuel Purchas's wife.

The central panel of the window shows a full length figure of Samuel Purchas, the face being a copy of a portrait in his book. He wears a cassock with ruff and stands on a grassy mound with trees on either side, for Eastwood. The left hand window shows the shield of Saint Laurence, followed by that of Westminster Abbey and Richard Hakluyt who was buried there. The three crowns are from the arms of Bristol Cathedral, followed by The Virginia Company. Cockethurst Farm is shown as it was in the 1970's, with one of Vassal's ships at the bottom.

At the head of the central window Saint John's College Cambridge is depicted along with the emblem of Saint John the Baptist for Thaxted Church and again the entwined initials of Jane Lease. At the base of this panel is text explaining the purpose of the window.

The right-hand window shows the arms of Captain John Smith, followed by a shield relating to the second part of the dedication of this church "All Saints". There are the arms of the New England Council, Archbishop George Abbot and John King, the Bishop of London. The panel finishes with a shield for Saint Martin's of Ludgate Hill.

The East Window

The Chancel is small, only 29 ft x 16ft. The roof is 14th Century, with braced collar beams; the two tie beams are moulded. The chancel arch is 14th Century and above it are marks of an earlier roof. Below the arch are two ends of the rood beam which was sawn off. There are no signs of a rood stair case.

Photograph of centre panel of reredos through squint

The Nave was the original Norman Church, and one of the original windows can be seen in the North wall whilst traces of two others are also still visible. There were probably three in each wall. The Roof is 15th Century work with massive tie beams. Four of the trusses have octagonal crown posts of unusual workmanship for a village church. When the roof was retiled in 1935, the 7" x 7" beams were as sound as when they were first placed there. Before the altar is the 18th Century tomb of the Vassal family, former owners of Cockethurst Farm, and an effigy in brass of Thomas Burroughs dated 1600.

The old vicarage in Eastwoodbury Lane, (Glebe House), had over the 19th century deteriorated until in the 1930's it was not thought possible to be adequate as a home for a family.

Eastwood Church choir at Jennifer Clark's wedding

The Barn - Eastwood's former church hall taken in 1938, possible Empire Day

Mr. Fowler made a suggestion that he would finance the building of a suitable new vicarage and church hall in exchange for a parcel of glebe land which could be used as a water meadow on the ground now taken up by the Laurence Industrial unit which butts up to the site of the hall.

The church hall, next to the entrance to Glebe House

The Vicarage has been a family home to a number of vicars and their families since 1937 and the gardens have been used for fetes and various out-door functions, as well as being a well-cared for garden for the rest of the year When the new road joining the lane with the A127 was built, a wall was placed around the property to help to shield it from the noise of traffic.

GEORGINA EMMA SPENCER

When information was being collected for the Project Eastwood Exhibition that was scheduled to take place in June 2000, we were fortunate enough to receive help from various sources. One of those calls came from a Lady who lives in Leigh and was looking for help herself with a project that she was working on. Her name is Jean Willis and together with her Daughter Sue she was looking for information regarding the wife of one of the Vicars of Eastwood called John Spencer.

Jean had found a note book which enclosed a calling card on which was the name "Mrs John Spencer, Eastwood Vicarage"

The south aisle window

We were able to confirm that there was indeed a Vicar of Saint Laurence and All Saints Church Eastwood, whose name was John Spencer. He was Vicar from 1867 to 1900. Jean looked for information on the Census' nearest to 1867 to check whether there was a wife on record. In 1871 the Census showed a wife, Margaret, however, in the 1881 Census, the Vicar was shown as a Widower and lived in Southend, in a lodging house in Clifftown Road. The 1891 Census, showed both the Revd John Spencer and his wife Georgina. Therefore the notebook must belong to her. Their wedding took place at Sutton Church in 1883, on the 6th of February and the Marriage Certificate gave us quite a lot of information. The bride, whose maiden name was Crampton, was married by her Father, Josiah, who was Vicar of Sutton. The Groom's Father was a Brewer! The two witnesses were later traced as Reverend Spencer's son W.E Spencer and Andrew Noble William Bredin the Rector of Sutton and the Husband of the Reverend Josiah Crampton's youngest Daughter, Pamela. It does get even more complicated, as Reverend Josiah himself, married Florence, the Daughter of Andrew Noble Bredin, a wife younger than two of her Step Daughters.

Josiah died only a month after performing the marriage of John & Georgina; perhaps the relief of marrying off three of his four daughters being too much for him. His tombstone records that he was the Grandson of the Surgeon General of Ireland, which title died out with Josiah.

OTHER CHURCH-RELATED BUILDINGS

The Church Hall has been in constant use since it was first built. It has both a small and a large hall, with kitchens, and a stage between. The activities that have been taking place over the last sixty-plus years, include Badminton Club, Art Club, Craft Club, The St. Laurence Stage Players, Brownies, Cubs, Scouts, family parties, Church Holiday Club, and Pre-school. In addition, fetes, plant sales, musical evenings, jumble sales and dog training also take place; it is also used as a venue for wedding receptions for local couples.

'The Glebe' or 'Glebe House', the former vicarage

Prior to work being carried out to straighten the brook from Cockethurst to the rear of the Churchyard, the brook actually ran in front of the Vicarage, Hall, and Glebe House, which were approached across individual bridges.

Georgina Spencer's notebook contains a great deal of information that any Vicar's wife would find useful; a list of the people with whom the Reverend and Mrs Spencer would socialise; recipes collected from friends; information on certain functions that took place within the Parish; an advertisement for a servant, knitting patterns, etc.

The various notes contained in the book show something of the character of a Victorian lady, who was brought up in a privileged home and whose interests were very much in keeping with those circumstances, such as music and painting. Georgina had a strong sense of duty which has been borne out by her work in the parish, such as her twice weekly visits with her husband to the village school and also to see various parishioners who were either elderly, or infirm. The beautiful East window at St. Laurence and all Saints, mentions John Spencer and the painted reredos behind the altar was given to the church in his memory, by Georgina.

The current Vicarage

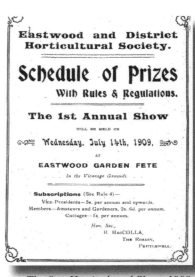

The first Horticultural Show, 1909

Eastwood Carnival 1956

During the time it took to do the research for 'Project Eastwood', many of the local people who knew Eastwood well, were encouraged to write their memories down for our archive. This chapter is dedicated to them, with thanks for all their hard work, and it remains exactly as it was written for us.

Eastwoodbury Lane

Wells Avenue

Gun Emplacement

Houses opposite church

My lasting memory of Eastwoodbury Lane is one of tranquillity. I used to cycle along the road to deliver newspapers to the houses, cottages and smallholdings along the way. The occupants of one of the houses opposite the church had two rather ferocious dogs, which barked aggressively from behind the closed front door, as one terrified little girl pushed the papers quickly through the letter box and beat a hasty retreat. There were not many dwellings along the Lane; there were mostly fields and smallholdings from where it was possible to buy eggs, fresh vegetables and flowers.

My mother used to take my brother Max and I to visit my aunt and cousin Janet who lived in Wells Avenue. I can remember the three of us playing on and around a large concrete gun emplacement which stood on a plot of land around a huge pylon in Eastwoodbury Lane. As children we were unaware of the significance of this building as we had been evacuated to Derbyshire during the war. At the age of ten, it was just great fun to scramble on top of it and view the world from on high.

At the end of the war my aunt and cousin were living in a bungalow which backed on to the airport. The perimeter was surrounded by a high wire fence, with barbed wire on top. My uncle had been a prisoner of war, and on his return was horrified at the sight of the fence at the end of his garden. It brought back too many unpleasant memories. Shortly after, the family moved to another part of Southend.

Yvonne Blackbarrow (nee Hofman) - June 2000

Eastwood School .

Leighfields Road

Leighfields Avenue

Greengrocery round

Bellhouse Lane, (now Bellhouse Raod)

Leonard and Alice Bridges came to live in Eastwood in the mid 1920's. They bought a plot of land, 70 feet by 120 feet, for £35 in the early 1930's on the corner of Leighfields Avenue and what is now Leighfields Road. I was born there in 1934. Our garden was large, with fruit and plum trees and Leonard grew vegetables.

Len Bridges with his horse and cart

He started a greengrocery round with horse and cart. The horse was stabled at the bottom of the garden. Wholesale suppliers brought sacks of vegetables and boxes of fruit which were stored in a shed until needed for distribution.

Six days a week Leonard set off on his round to roads in Leigh and Eastwood. The horse quickly learnt at which houses he was to stop. The working day was a long one, but unhurried, as greengrocer and customer would engage in a friendly chat.

At the beginning of the war we spent a few months in West Hanningfield and my father continued his regular round, coming back to the rented bungalow in Hanningfield each night.

My sister and I went to Eastwood School and our father continued his greengrocery business as well as undertaking ARP duties at night. He retired in the early 1960's. Alice died in 1966 and Leonard in 1973, aged 80 years.

Daphne Bridges

Len and Alice Bridges

28

Springwater Road

Gravel Road

Midwife and Nurse

My father, George Cousins Podger was born in Somerset in 1897. Shortly after his father died in 1897 he decided to move to Eastwood to be near relations. So in 1903/4 he and his mother, a nurse and midwife, moved to Springwater Road, where he became a local builder.

In 1911 he served a 5-year apprenticeship with Mr C H J Talmage of Southend.

During the First World War he served as an engineer in the Royal Flying Corps at a base in Scotland from 1916 to 1919. When he returned to Eastwood in 1920, he married Sarah Snell and he continued his building career and built thirteen bungalows in Springwater Road and seven in Gravel Road, Eastwood, between 1936 and 1961. He also repaired a lot of war-damaged properties in Eastwood and surrounding areas.

He was forced to retire in 1961 due to ill health but remained in his bungalow in Springwater Road until his death in 1982 at the age of 86.

Beryl Bridge

Nurse Podger's son - George

Egg production

Eastwoodbury Lane

Ack-Ack (anti-aircraft) gun

World War Two

I suppose one of my earliest recollections was of going every Sunday to Braintree to pick up eggs for the farm from my aunt. Also we visited my grandmother and grandfather, my mother's parents. As Grandfather kept a pub, nothing started until about 10.00pm as the pub shut. I was put to sleep on the back seat of our car, and eventually arrived home about 1.00am and Father would carry me into bed. Certainly until I was about 8 years old I remember very little about the journey home, only being woken up to get out of the car and stagger up to bed.

We had an Ack-Ack gun at the bottom of our land towards St Laurence Church, which certainly during the first years of the war saw quite a lot of action although whether it hit anything was probably in some doubt. Meanwhile I would stand on one of the pigsty roofs to watch the German aircraft on their way to London and their return. One of the things to collect in those days was shrapnel; better still if it was hot. One could exchange it for different shapes!

Also right outside our gate was a check point where passes were checked. If you wished to go into Southend, no pass, no go! As schoolboys, we did try it on, having no pass, we wouldn't be able to go to school, but it didn't work, as the police knew all the boys who were going to school. It was very busy for about nine months in the run up to D-Day. One winter when the snow was quite deep all my friends and I spent about a week sledging down Southbourne Grove. Sledges were built by various soldiers who seemed to have plenty of spare time.

I knew the Church Wardens at St Lawrence Church quite well and as a youngster used to hear the conversations. One of their hopes was that the church would be bombed and then there would be no need to worry about repairs; their prayers were never answered!

Bob Bull (Thanet Grange)

Eastwoodbury Lane - January 1947

Lane between Church and Bury Farm going to the Wilderness Farm

Bury Cottages

Farming work

Harvest Festival

Fire at Westborough (West Barrow)

Eastwoodbury Lane

The Police Box

Sunday school and the Misses Fowler

Silver Jubilee

Airport

John Bullock, my father, lived in Bury Cottages for many years and worked as a stockman with a herd of Friesian dairy cows for Mr Watts of Bury Farm, which was situated opposite the Church. As well as caring for the cattle, he would also help on the land with the ploughing, harvesting, thatching, hedging and ditching. When Mr Watts gave up the farm, he worked for Mr Hurst of Rochford Hall, who continued with the herd which were still kept in the cattle sheds that were part of the farm buildings opposite Bury Priory.

Dad's hobby was to grow pumpkins and other vegetables which he would give to the church to display at Harvest Festival time. He retired from the farm at the age of 78. We have a photograph which shows him trying to control a fire in the stables at West Barrow Hall in the early 1960's Bury Cottages.

I was born in Bury Cottages, which stand at the end of the main runway of Southend Airport. My earliest memory is of walking the one and a half miles to Eastwood School along Eastwoodbury Lane and into Snakes Lane - no public transport in those days! The lane was very narrow and winding with grass verges and lots of wild flowers. From the Church to Cockethurst Farm there were farm cottages, some of which were thatched.

Pillar Box and Tea Tree Cottages on the north side of Eastwoodbury Lane

One of the special things that many children would like about where I lived, was that almost on the bend in the road there was an old-fashioned blue Police box, which nowadays would be a major part of the Dr. Who series on TV - 'The Tardis'

Our Sunday School was held in the grounds of the old vicarage (Glebe House) until the new Church Hall was built and opened. The Sunday School was run by the Misses Fowler. We had summer fetes held in the meadow round Cockethurst Farm and outings to Maldon, Clacton and Frinton.

I can remember the Silver Jubilee of King George VI and Queen Elizabeth in 1937; a street party was organised with games, races and fancy dress.

I recall war being declared; some families moved away and the military moved in to the empty houses. The airport became a fighter base; Pill Boxes, Tank Traps and barbed wire appeared.. Some of the footpaths were closed. There was a 'Dig For Victory' campaign and every spare piece of ground was cultivated. Even the parks were dug up - the flower beds were replaced with vegetables.

My family lived on a farm and I had to take my turn at fire-watching. Peace came in 1945 and we attended a thanksgiving service at the Church and life got back to normal again.

I was married in Eastwood Church in 1949; then I moved to Rochford.

Eileen Brown (nee Bullock)

Was this a Church outing?

32

Street Party organised by Mrs L. Anderson in Croft Close, south of Coombes Corner in 1945 to celebrate the end of WWII.

Shirley Road

Waterworks Road

Mr Fowler

Brickfields

Shop names and owners

Dairymen

Oakwood Club/Pub

Ned Ford

Edward's Hall

Farms and farmers

We were a large family. My mother had ten children and we lived in Shirley Road, off Waterworks Road. In 1929, all the roads were unmade. We attended Eastwood School, and I was in Miss Morton's class who taught the infants. Mr Fowler, a Justice of the Peace, drove to the school in a pony and trap. We would line up in the playground and he gave us an orange on Empire Day. A farthing (.083p) would buy a blackjack from Mr Hat's sweet shop next to the school. We walked across Arterial Road, down beside the rubber factory and the brickfields, through the field with the cows in next to the school.

The shops at the junction of Waterworks Road and Arterial Road were Chimes Store, Manns the Bakers and Banfields. About this time in the early 1930's the rubber factory burnt down. My father worked for Howard's Dairies at Station Road in Leigh, and my sister and I used to take him his dinner in a basin.

We moved to No 5, Tudor Road and then to No 9 Bosworth Road, Eastwood in 1933, and the rent was £1. 1s (one pound, one shilling, approximately one pound and five pence.) We walked to school passing brick kilns burning at Cornish's Brickfield opposite Dandies Drive and Gale's Brickfield (now called Hudson Road) up Lambeth Road. The air was thick with the smell of sulphur from the burning kilns.

Rochford Corner, where the parade of shops is now, was a field that people took a shortcut across. During the Second World War this land was ploughed and grew crops, as was Eastwood Park and Oakwood Park under the direction of Mr H. H. Smith, a local farmer. Our local shops were at Jones' Corner, a busy local shopping place. Mr and Mrs Joy's chemist shop was here where you bought medicine and Mr Joy would treat you for free. If you could not afford to pay, he gave the medicine as well. People used to go to him for help with their ailments. A very kind and generous man indeed - he lived in a bungalow opposite his shop and kept bees.

Mr Wilson had the garage and sold bicycles. W.E. Jones sold wool, cottons and all needlework requirements. Mr Gulliver had Lilliput Garage and charged accumulators as did Mr Usher. Mr Walker was the butcher, and his shop was opposite the Bell House pub. The Post Office was on the corner of Dandies Drive, and the grocer's shop was opposite 'Alldays' (later the Co-op).

There were two policemen in Eastwood, Mr Fletcher and Mr Bunn, who lived a little way up Bellhouse Lane.

The fish and chip shop was at the bottom of Eastwood Rise, run by Mr and Mrs Garside and their son, John. John Garside helped to run Eastwood Rovers, the local football team. Mr Braybrooke had his newspaper shop where the car park is now and to the left of Mr Braybrooke's shop stood a railway carriage where a Mrs Underwood sold second-hand clothes. Where the BP garage is now there stood some cottages where Mr and Mrs Jollye lived, the local farmer and his wife. Next to them was Harris's scrap yard and a little shop called 'Grimwade Stores'.

On the other side of the road was Weston Stores which sold everything. When they were closed you knocked on the door and bought your bits and pieces. Water was sold for 1d (half a penny) a bucket - not everyone was lucky enough to have mains water. Behind the shop was an orchard, where Goodhew later built Springwater Close.

The Oakwood Club where the Oakwood Pub is now was a much smaller building. On the corner of Eastwood Rise was Burchill's Off Licence and Backholer's the greengrocers. Opposite the Oakwood Club was the fish shop and Mr Booth's shop who sold buttons, wool, cotton and cloth. He rode around on his trade bike selling his wares.

The 'Silver Jubilee' replaced this building which was Weston's Stores'

Going west along Rayleigh Road on the left we used to pass Granville House, the waterworks driveway and a sign reading Victoria Road - but no road, just a plank across the ditch. Where Nestuda Flats are now, there used to be a blacksmith's shop owned by Ned Ford - a great character who would turn his hand to any job; shoe your horse, mend your bike, repair your kettle, build your cart or wagon, repair your car. Indeed a man of many talents. Ned Ford was a gentle and very generous man who helped a lot of people in Eastwood. Ned lived with his wife and daughter in a bungalow across from his yard.

At the bottom of Eastwood Rise near Wagstaff's old brickfield was a little shop run by Mrs Kinnaid. There was also a Catholic Church on the corner of Hillside road and Eastwood Rise - this church was well attended.

Edwards Hall, a farm of seventy-five acres, situated on the south side of the Roach valley has seen many changes. Before the Second World War, Mr Adlam kept cows and had a milk round. Some fields were covered in broom bushes; others such as Bosworth Road field were covered in gorse and hawthorn bushes. Tudor Road field had some deep holes where sand had been excavated to build Bosworth and Tudor Road bungalows. The Second World War changed things; Mr H. H. Smith who was farming 'Flemmings', took over the farm. Each field was cleared of bushes and trees. Hedges were trimmed back; trees were lopped to let in air, ditches dug out. The land was then ploughed and sown - a tremendous task for a small farm. The field where the Fever Hospital stood at the side of Pond Field in Green Lane, off Dandies Drive was also cleaned and cultivated after the hospital was demolished. Lower Edwards Hall, the south side of Rayleigh Road, now Progress Road, was farmed by Mr Timewell who also farmed at Rayleigh Weir.

Mrs Richens had the farm at the top of Nobles Green, where she kept cows and pigs. Mr Fowler farmed Dandies Farm, now western Approaches, and he also kept cows. Before the war there were several milkmen; Mr Adlam of Edwards Hall, Mrs Snell of New England Farm, Mr Durell of Dawes Heath, Mr Flack of Eastwood Road, Rayleigh, the Co-op and Howard's Dairies

Sid Broomfield -April 2000

Another local character, who must have worked all his life on the local farms was Bob Clover, who featured briefly in the limelight in 1978 through an exhibition of drawings featured in the local library, depicting his life and his work.

Eastwood — this was your life

By Louise Dray

PEOPLE of Eastwood, this was your life, half a century ago. Old Bob Clover, now in his seventies, wanted to be an artist as a young man but education and opportunities weren't what they are now. He had to work on local farms instead.

Now, suddenly, he looks like being famous locally.

A librarian and a vicar want to put his work on show.

Bob's been painting memories of life of those days —

when the Eastwood area was mainly made up of farms. And he's been 'discovered' by a young local couple, Colin and Jean Hall, of Orchard Side.

Jean said: "We told the vicar of our enthusiasm about the paintings and he suggested putting them on exhibition in the church — St. Laurence's. But he and my husband agreed the library would reach a wider audience."

Librarian Nick Fewster, responsible for Eastwood from Rayleigh district, is very interested.

"I'm just getting formal permission but there is enough material there for display stands in the Kent Elms library," he said.

"I think local people of all the mixed age groups we get will find it fascinating."

As for Old Bob, he recalls: "We got sixpence a day for rook scaring with rattles and scarecrows."

He recollects not only the great oaks that grew in Eastwood in the last century but the way the pigs were fattened for market by letting

them eat the acorns that dropped beneath.

He's clear on exactly how the great shire horses were 'tacked up' for work. One page of drawings details every bit of harness equipment put on them.

A "hard, wet, dirty" job that needed sack aprons was mangold pulling. Dung spreading was "tiring, filthy, and smelly," he recalls.

But the young man who wanted to be an artist studied the different textures of the earth made by ploughing, and the patterns made by the cutting of crops.

Now his raw studies will give pleasure to thousands.

Southend Standard - September 27th, 1978

36

Cottage names

People living nearby

Daily life in the 1930's and 1940's

I was born in Tea Tree Cottage in 1936, then after that we moved across to Workhouse Cottages.

Tea Tree Cottage

When I think of my childhood days, there are so many things that I like to remember. We lived on the Cockethurst Farm Estate, at No 2, Workhouse Cottages, which was owned by Mr and Mrs Fowler.

My father was a horseman on the farm in those days and used to start work at 6am. My mother worked on the farm, too; after getting my brother and me up early for school, she would then go into the fields herself. This was hard work as everything had to be done by hand; not very much machinery unlike today and the conditions that we lived in were not at all modern by today's standards. We had an outside toilet at the bottom of the garden and no running water; we had to pump water up from the well.

You can imagine how hard it was to do the weekly washing. Many times I would come home after school to see Mum doing the washing in an old tin bath, then taking it to be boiled. My job was to push it down with a copper stick, then to help with rinsing it, adding a blue bag to make it pure white.

We used the tin bath to bathe in and of course all the water had to be fetched, carried and heated in the copper. Although these were hard times indeed, we didn't know any different; it was our way of life and we had lots of happy times in the cottage.

I remember Les and Margaret Timewell's shop opposite the Church. My Mum, Mrs Doe used the shop for everything when we lived at Workhouse Cottages and it was either my brother Dennis or I that had to get the shopping. I remember that when the War ended in 1945, my Mum sent me to get red, white and blue ribbons for my hair.

Also, just opposite Cockethurst Farm, where Mr and Mrs Fowler lived with their daughters, there was a little humpback bridge that led into the stack-yard field. Here Mr Keeling would bring their thrashing machine to cut the corn, oats and barley. From then on, the men on the farm would stack it and use some to thatch hay stacks, and the two cottages down the lane, Tea Tree and Pillar Box cottages.

Timewell's shop, opposite the church

As a child I was given 3d a week for collecting all the eggs that the chickens had laid. I did this after school every day, 5 days a week, and was glad to get the money at the end of the week from Mrs Fowler.

Further down the lane was a small farm cottage where Mr and Mrs Overall lived, and beyond that another black boarded cottage where Mr and Mrs Nunn lived.

Part of the 'Project Eastwood' group. Sheila Currie is centre front, John Bird, who provided many photographs, far right

My day started by walking up the dusty road into Snakes Lane which had high hedges each side of the road, and was very narrow, with lots of bends. We walked all the way to Eastwood School. When I came home for our dinner we would sometimes have rabbit stew; my Dad would have caught the rabbit the day before. I will always remember that smell. Then it would be the long trek back to school for more lessons. When the bell finally went, we were very pleased and I can remember running home as fast as I could. My job then was to feed the chickens. My Mum would have boiled the potato peelings for me to mix with a handful of corn for each chicken; it was more like fun than work. I remembered each one of their names, so I liked doing it.

After tea, my friend Sonny Kindred would come round to call and we might play whips and tops. We would whip our tops so hard that the string was all frayed!

We had no TV, of course so we would listen to the radio. Dick Barton was our favourite. Sometimes the radio would go dead as the batteries had to be recharged. We had no such thing as electricity, only gas mantles for lighting downstairs; upstairs we could carry a candle to show the way, and being a small child I can remember it being quite scary as it was so dark outside, because of the shortage of street lighting. But I would say my prayers, cover my head and fall asleep.

For us, Christmas was a special time, even though it really was Christmas Day in the Workhouse! Although we didn't have much money, we had a proper Christmas Dinner; cockerels, which had been fattened up and Christmas puddings which Mum had made. We children were very excited because we were each allowed to stir the mixture and have a wish. Then we would put silver threepenny pieces in, hoping that we would be lucky enough to have one in our piece when it was served up. These puddings were made well in advance of Christmas, which Mum said added to the flavour.

On Christmas Eve we would put our decorations up. These were mainly balloons and paper chains, which we had made ourselves. We had a lot of fun with these, as they stretched right across to each corner of the room. We did this while Mum and Auntie got everything ready for the next day. Dad and my uncle would go to the local pub, which in those days was The Cock Inn, at the bottom of Cherry Orchard Lane. If we were lucky we might get a packet of crisps, which in those days had a twist of blue paper in which the salt was placed. When they returned we were washed and put to bed. I remember going up the stairs where there were no lights, only a candle and night light to carry up. The stairs and bedrooms were pitch-black. I used to get into bed as quickly as possible and pull the sheets over my head.

Sheila Currie lived at No 2 Workhouse Cottages

In the morning as soon as I saw the light coming in through the window, I would jump up, and then look into my pillow case to see if there was anything inside. Father Christmas had called and there were fruit, sweets and probably some books and pencils. Just little things really, but I do remember once having a lovely doll; she was made with a rag body and celluloid arms, legs and head. I was thrilled to bits. A lady called Mrs Nunn, who lived further down the lane, had kindly brought me a pram for my doll. I was very lucky that Christmas.

As the morning went on, Mum and Auntie would get on with the dinner. The table was set with a starched white tablecloth and I could remember the lovely smell of roast chicken and Christmas pudding from the kitchen.

After dinner, when the washing up had been done, (and that meant a big, boiling kettle of water as we had no hot water!) we would settle down. The grown-ups would have a nap, whilst we children would play with our toys.

Later on in the evening, we would play cards or games of some sort, sometimes we would just listen to something on the radio. We children were very happy with our toys and of course the lovely food. The next day was Boxing Day and we would all go over to my Aunt's and Uncle's and have another lovely day at their house.

Sheila Currie (nee Doe)

St. Laurence Players' First production

41

Local police

Although hailing from Coventry, Bill Fletcher moved to Eastwood and joined the Southend Constabulary in April 1930 and after three months training became a Police Constable. As part of his commitment to his work, Bill obtained a certificate in First Aid from St Johns and took a Royal Life Saving Certificate course.

In January, 1938 the Royal Society for Prevention of Cruelty to Animals acknowledged his courage and humanity, when he rescued a horse from a brook near Rayleigh Road.

As one of the Eastwood Bobbies who cycled round Eastwood, Bill kept an eye on what was going on in the area. He became a well-known member of the community, which included the gypsy families who lived here. Always a friendly person, Bill loved to speak to everyone from the children through to the pensioners.

A family man, Bill met his wife Alice in Coventry and they were married at St. Thomas, Kersley and Coundon on 24th October, 1932. A parishioner of St Laurence and All Saints, it was there that he and his wife celebrated both their Gold and Diamond wedding Anniversaries. The couple had 3children, 3 grandchildren and 3 great-grandchildren.

In 1953, Bill was chosen, together with other members of the local force, to be on parade at the march-past for the coronation of Queen Elizabeth II. For this he was awarded the Queen's Medal.

In 1955, he completed 25 years in the Southend Borough Constabulary. The picture was taken to mark the occasion. His years in the force saw a great deal of change in the area, particularly in the volume of traffic. During his time in the force, he worked hard to establish a recreation club for the members and was made an honorary member on his retirement. He continued to enjoy the club for the rest of his life.

SOUTHEND STANDARD

Bill was among the first of Eastwood's police...

ONE of Southend and Essex's oldest public servants died on Friday September 5, aged 95.

William Fletcher — known as Bill to his friends — was the Chief Bailiff of Essex when he retired from his Chelmsford-based duties in 1973.

He first worked as a bailiff at the Southend County Court, following his retirement from the town's police force in 1955. He'd been a policeman for 25 years.

Bill's son, Maurice, explained: "He moved to Eastwood more or less when it was opened up to be policed — in other words, when the area became a regular beat."

Bill joined the police in 1930 and married his beloved Agnes in 1932.

They moved from their Leigh flat to a house in Rayleigh Road, Eastwood, in 1933 — where they lived for the rest of their lives.

After the war, Bill worked at Leigh police station. His career was rewarded with three medals, including one for exemplary police service.

"He was a great fan of snooker and billiards," Maurice added, "and was the champion at the Police Club.

"We still worked together on the allotment until he was 82."

Agnes passed away in

Public servant — Bill was one of the first policemen to work the Eastwood beat

1999, aged 93. Bill kept up his commitments after that and was on parade with old comrades, for a celebration outside the town's main Victoria Avenue police station, just a year ago.

He leaves three children, three grandchildren and the same number of great-grandchildren

His funeral will be held at Eastwood's St Laurence Church next Wednesday, September 24 at 2pm.

All friends are welcome and relatives have asked for family flowers only.

All donations should be given to the church via the Co-op.

The blacksmith

H.E. 'Ned' Ford

Ned was the village blacksmith; he grew up in Eastwood although his father came from Kent. His father built the forge and family home on the land where Nestuda House now stands. Ned was born early in the 20th Century and followed his father into the family business.

He became a man with a multitude of skills and adapted over the years to the many changes. His early life was centred on the working horse, and he could not only shoe the horses, but repair cart wheels, horse-drawn vehicles and various farm implements.

In the early 1950's he shod the racing horses belonging to H H Smith and these animals were in complete contrast to the heavy farm horse. Later in life, with the changes from using heavy horses for farm work to using machinery, most of the horses he shod were for riding. He adapted to the times and became a largely self-taught mechanic and paint sprayer. He was able to build a wooden-framed horse box on a lorry chassis. There was not much in the practical world that Ned could not turn his hand to and he was fully employed by the local farmers and haulage contractors. He would greet people with a grunt and would often turn away muttering, but he would rarely turn down someone's cry for help when they were in a muddle or something was broken. He would work late into the evening or on a Sunday to get a machine or lorry ready for work on a Monday morning.

It was a great blow to Ned when in the early 1970's Southend Borough Council put a compulsory purchase order on his premises as part of a grand scheme to modernise. Nothing was built on the site for several years, adding salt to the wound for Ned. And so, one of the last proper brick-built forges, complete with leather bellows, was consigned to history.

Despite his gruff and rather awe-inspiring manner, Ned would delight in showing a young lad some of the skills of the forge and would get them pumping the bellows, but not too much or they would get a bellow of a different kind! He must have had a good sense of humour also, as he took the village by surprise by buying a new pink Vauxhall car!

Ned married a Miss Grant and they had one daughter. They lived in a bungalow called Blossomfield on the other side of the Rayleigh Road. Ned, in contrast to his near-contemporary, Sonny Jollye, would often find time for a holiday with friends or a cruise with his wife, and also enjoyed a visit to The Oakwood on most days. He was a much-loved and well-respected member of the community, someone who is still remembered with affection today.

Ned Ford

Ned Ford's yard

43

Farm work

Harold Jollye, known as Sonny or simply Jollye, was an agricultural contractor and farmer living in Eastwood for many years. His father had a reputation as a rather austere man, and was said to be the son of a well-connected Lincolnshire doctor, but he himself was thought to be the black sheep of the family. He had come to Essex at the end of the 19th Century in reduced circumstances and had taken employment as a horseman and groom in Shoebury.

Sonny was born about 1907, and grew up in Eastwood. He became a hard-working and very astute man, yet he could barely read or write. In his younger days, he had had a serious accident with a mower which left him with a permanent leg injury, which later resulted in an amputation. It was remarkable that Jollye was able to carry out farm work with such a disability. His early life was with working horses, and he progressed to working with tractors during the War. He was an important part of the Eastwood rural scene for over 50 years, carrying out contracting work on many of the small farms now long gone.

Sonny had the good fortune to sell his land on the corner of Eastwood Rise and Springwater for building in the early 1960's which allowed him to buy Great Wasketts Farm near Crays Hill. He still continued a lot of work around Eastwood and could offer virtually all farming services from the plough to combine harvester.

He was a blunt man who did not mince his words, but he did have a good sense of humour. He never drove a car, but went everywhere by tractor, often perched on the back on a hessian sack with his good leg on the draw bar to stop him from falling off. He said this was his idea of 'chauffeur-driven'! He continued to work into his late 70's until poor health got the better of him and towards the end was even lifted on to the tractor to go rolling the land. He died in 1989 at the age of 82. He never married, but his late housekeeper, Phyllis Thompson, implied that he had had a tough childhood and had been expected to work hard from a very early age. Perhaps this coloured his outlook on life, for he seemed to have very little time for anything but hard work throughout his life.

Sonny Jollye early 60's

Health visitor

School nurse

For 25 years, Joyce served as Health visitor and school nurse, a job which involved visiting families with young children, running infant welfare clinics and antenatal clinics, teaching mothercraft in school and clinic, running head inspections in the schools (an occupation always earning the title of "Nitty Nora!") and working in school clinics dealing with immunisation, warts and school medicals.

The infant welfare clinics were held twice a month in the Baptist Church Hall and rapidly increased to weekly, then twice each week! It soon became clear that the hall was not big enough and a purpose built clinic was necessary.

Kent Elms Clinic was built at the same time as the library and provided improved facilities and increased staffing levels for ante-natal, post natal, infant welfare, mother craft classes and school clinic.

Joyce is well known for her work with the St John's Ambulance Brigade, in which she holds the position of President of the Southend-on-sea combined Division. After completing her nursing training at Southend General Hospital, she entered St John's as a Nursing Officer in 1956.

Christmas Eve, 1943, Joyce was called up for wartime service with the WAAF, and her place of work was RAF Headquarters at what we called the 'bombed flats' – the flats at the junction of Oaken Grange Drive and Manners Way. The airmen's mess was situated at the Medway Knitting factory just off Prince Avenue, near today's Tesco store.

Joyce married Gordon Kipling in 1970, and thereafter lived in Eastwood.

Joyce Kipling (SRN,CMB Pt 1.HVCert, O.S.St.John)

AGM of St John's

Joyce is honoured

45

Eastwood Old Road

St David's

The Mission

Eastwood School

Airborne Industries

Farming

Shops

In January, 1940, we went to live in Eastwood Old Road, near its junction with the Fairway. The parish church was a long way away, so we went to 'The Mission', where St David's is now. The Mission was a converted barn, furnished with large, heavy pews from another church, and a harmonium.

There was a service at 6.30pm on Sundays, taken by Mr Arnold, the lay reader, who also played the organ.

St david's Choir - cica 1946

After a few weeks, my mother (Mrs Ida Mitchell) offered to take over the organ and later the church acquired a bigger organ which was pumped by hand. Later my mother took charge of the Sunday School.

We walked to The Mission across the fields, where the Progress Road Industrial Estate is now.

When the Lay reader was called up into the army, my grandfather – Mr E.S. Tutton - got permission from the Bishop to take the evening service. Grandma made him a cassock from an old coat and a surplice from a sheet!

The Sunday School became very large when the little 'tin chapel' near Jones' Corner closed. My mother ran a club for the older girls and later started a choir.

After the War ended, Mum, my sister and I started going to morning service at St Laurence's and sang in the choir. The highlights of the year were the Nativity Play and the Good Friday music. We sang 'Olivet to Calvary' by Maunder and Stainer's 'Crucifixion' on alternate years. There was also a choir social at which I seem to remember the same people singing the same solos each year!

Eastwoodbury Lane

I attended Eastwood School from 1940 to 1945 apart from the one-and-a-half years when the school was evacuated. It was a long way from our end of the parish, so we had to take lunch at first. Later we could buy a meal (I think they were British Restaurant meals at a cost of one penny for each course; soup, dinner and pudding. Much later, meals were cooked in the new dining room.

My lasting memory of school was sitting in the air-raid shelter, often for long periods because of the frequency of air raids. I remember the smell of the wet clay and the noise of water squelching under the duck boards as we moved along. It was too dark to read, but we learnt a lot of spellings and mental arithmetic, and sometimes sang.

Picture of the 'Woodcutters'

I remember being told by the headmaster that if there was as air raid on the way to school, we should return home if we were less than half-way. We used to walk slowly for the first half, in hope of being able to go home, and then run the rest of the way to school.

We were allowed to use the footpath which ran behind the 'Balloon Factory' (later Airborne Industries' and came out near the school gate. This was considered safer than walking along the Arterial Road which was the main landmark followed by enemy planes.

Johnny's Hardware, Rayleigh Road - Formerly Second Post Office and Telephone Exchange and Weston's General Stores

Sometimes it was possible to pick up pieces of scrap balloon fabric, which made good strong shopping bags and gas mask cases. I still have a pencil case made of it, containing 'utility brand' pencils.

The Eastwood School building was very modern, having been completed just before the war. We had a fully equipped gym and a cookery room. We had lessons on how to use up leftover food. I vividly remember making parsnip fritters, because a lot of the girls didn't like them and I ate too many! My old cookery notebook begins every recipe with the words, 'Re-constitute the dried egg...'!

The headmaster at that time was Mr Fortescue. He was a wonderful head and only made one school rule – 'Be sensible'. I remember him coming to watch us country dancing and joining in with our teacher as his partner.

One major event in school during the war was 'The Book Drive'; we were encouraged to bring to school as many old books as possible to be sent as salvage to help the war effort. Anyone who brought one book was given a badge saying 'Private'. The more books you brought in, the higher the rank badge awarded. One girl got as far as Field Marshal. I wonder how many valuable old books were destroyed.

On the way home from school, we passed Mann's Bakery. If we had any money we could buy a 1d (one old penny) bag of yesterday's cakes or a slab of 'Nelson' which was rather like a piece of bread pudding with thin pastry top and bottom. I believe it was made out of stale cakes.

Soon after we arrived in Eastwood all the fields around us were ploughed up to grow food crops. Most of the field workers were women, apart from a few men too old to join the forces.

We children helped during the holidays and in the summer evenings. Picking up potatoes was a particularly back-breaking job. The very small potatoes, known as 'chats' were picked up separately as pig-food, and not regarded as good enough for humans. Spare potatoes were put into clamps and kept for the winter. We always enjoyed trailing in the summer. This involved standing up the stooks of wheat, barley, oats or rye in groups of 6 to let them dry. One hazard was that if the stooks were left lying down overnight there might be adders inside in the morning. The men killed the adders with sticks and hung them up on a tree – the old belief was that snakes did not die until sunset.

A lot of children missed school in the pea-picking season as this was piecework. I was not allowed to stay away from school. As my friend and I were too young to be employed the farmer sometimes gave us 3d or 6d pocket money.

When there was no work to do we played in the woods and fields. To help out the rations we picked blackberries and crab-apples and the owners of a big house in our road let us go into the orchard and pick up windfalls. If we got up at 5am we could pick mushrooms. We had to be early because other people picked them for sale to the shops. They were the very big field mushrooms and very tasty. At one time we were also asked to pick rose hips, which we took to school and we were paid, I think it was 3d a pound. They were needed to make syrup for babies.

Once a week we walked to the shops; the nearest were a quarter of an hour's walk away. We left the grocery order to be delivered. Milk, bread and greengrocery were delivered, all by horse and cart.

Apart from Church activities, there were no other places to go. We couldn't afford to go into Southend to the cinema and no-one was allowed on the beach.

Rita Mitchell

Avro Road

Earl's Hall School

Smallholdings Shops

Cockethurst Farm

The Misses Fowler

Fruit picking

The Cock Inn

Mr Fowler's funeral

Gun Emplacement

What I liked most about living in Avro Road was that there was a lot to keep you busy. I loved looking out of the window of my parents' bedroom because you could look over the hedge and see not only the church, but also Bury Priory, 'the big house'. I liked to walk past it in the spring when the little hollow at the side of the drive was full up with primroses, violets and bluebells. In the distance you could also see the fields to Big West; it was almost like living in the country.

Mrs Clark outside her Smallholding Shop

There were two main ways of getting about; on foot, or on a bike. Later, a bus service was introduced which terminated at Avro. This was the number 9, and although the route has been extended, the number has stayed the same.

The smallholdings in the lane were exciting places to visit, with lots of chickens, ducks and rabbits. I remember going with Mum to buy eggs from one smallholding that had an Alsatian dog who was able to tell if any of the birds was under the weather!

I was born at Avro Road, although I lived for most of my first year in East London, with my grandparents, as my mother was in hospital. During that time we were bombed out, and together with my aunts and uncles were dug out from the rubble of the building. We returned to Avro very dirty and scruffily dressed after our experiences.

I can remember going with Dad to Cockethurst Farm where we went into a big kitchen that was full of goodies and lovely smells. I was given some Turkish Delight. Sweets were still on ration, but there were always lots of things you could buy for a few pennies; liquorice wood, Ovaltine tablets, aniseed balls, Black Jacks and Fruit Salads could be purchased from Mrs Parson's little shop which was next to the smallholding where she lived in the lane.

In the summer we enjoyed going fruit picking and were able to earn pocket money. There was a bullace tree on the piece of land by Cart House Cottage. I loved to pick the bullaces and if there was enough, Mum would make some jam.

We would walk across the fields behind the church into Cherry Orchard Lane to The Cock Inn in Hall Road. My brother and I had a bottle of pop, while Mum and Dad had a drink before walking home again.

Sunday school was at the church hall and our teacher was Mrs Free who lived in Eastwoodbury Lane. The Misses Fowler would sometimes help and at special times would give us little Bible texts with pictures. My favourite one was at Mother's Day – it had a picture of the Queen on it. I gave this to Mum with a little bunch of flowers that they gave us at church.

Although I lived in Eastwoodbury, the nearest school at the time was Earl's Hall. Our lessons were held in an annexe that was part of Earl's Hall Baptist Church. Later we joined the main school building in Carlton Avenue. To get to school we walked to the part of Eastwoodbury Lane where the Smallholdings started and proceeded along a footpath between fields to Rochford Road and Feeches. From then on we walked towards The Bell, but up and over a big mound of earth that ended up as Prince Avenue School.

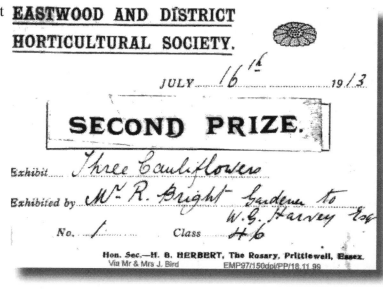

EASTWOOD AND DISTRICT HORTICULTURAL SOCIETY.

JULY 16ᵗʰ 19/3

SECOND PRIZE.

Exhibit _Three Cauliflowers_

Exhibited by _Mr R. Bright Gardener to W. G. Harvey Esq_

No. _1_   Class _H6_

Hon. Sec.—H. B. HERBERT, The Rosary, Prittlewell, Essex.
Via Mr & Mrs J. Bird   EMP97/150dpi/PP/16.11.99

I remember in 1947, the children in our road were invited into the house nearest the airport, where Miss Robinson lived, to watch Princess Elizabeth talking to us all from South Africa on her twenty-first birthday, and 6 years later, I was in London watching the Coronation on a black and white TV which came out a little green, even though it was only ten miles away from where we were!

When I started Senior School, I went to Eastwood and there the teachers were really good. Miss Rose taught history and even today I can remember the enthusiasm that she passed on to us all – history remains my favourite subject. Mr Collins was our art teacher and he taught us to enjoy what we could achieve, that we didn't always need to be the best. Mr Clegg was the teacher of RE. His stories from the Bible were inspirational. I was very pleased that in the fourth year I got the prize for the best exam result in the subject.

Workhouse Cottages, Eastwoodbury Lane.

As a teenager, I was allowed to join the church choir, which I enjoyed very much. The Fowler ladies used to come to church together in a big car and they would all wear exactly the same clothes, hats, shoes, bags and gloves. The daughters enjoyed singing, especially if there were any descants to a hymn. We were told to let them 'win' because it would look bad if we showed them up.

I can remember Mr Fowler's funeral at Eastwood church. There were so many important people there in splendid robes; the Mayor, Aldermen and Councillors all came to the service. There were always new flowers on his grave in a basket, every Sunday. I thought that they must have had a lot of money to be able to do this.

Our house was quite small compared to some, but we had three bedrooms. I had the smallest one even though my brother was younger. It was cosy with sunny yellow walls. Even in the winter, without central heating, it was warm. Downstairs there was a living room which had a range, but we later had this removed and a tiled fireplace put in so that we could have coal fires. We ate in the kitchen, and there was a big pantry to keep things cool. We also had a bathroom with a boiler which Mum could use to heat the water for washing. The toilet was outside the back door.

Because our area was next to a wartime airport, there were fortifications left over after the war finished. At the junction of Eastwoodbury Lane and Bristol Road there was a three-storey gun tower in which a Bofors gun stood. Once the gun was removed, it became a three-storey playground. Our parents were not too happy about this but it was difficult to stop us.

The area behind the council houses in the lane and those in the first half of Avro had a big area of concrete tank traps.

I lived in the area until my marriage in 1962.

Grace Panton

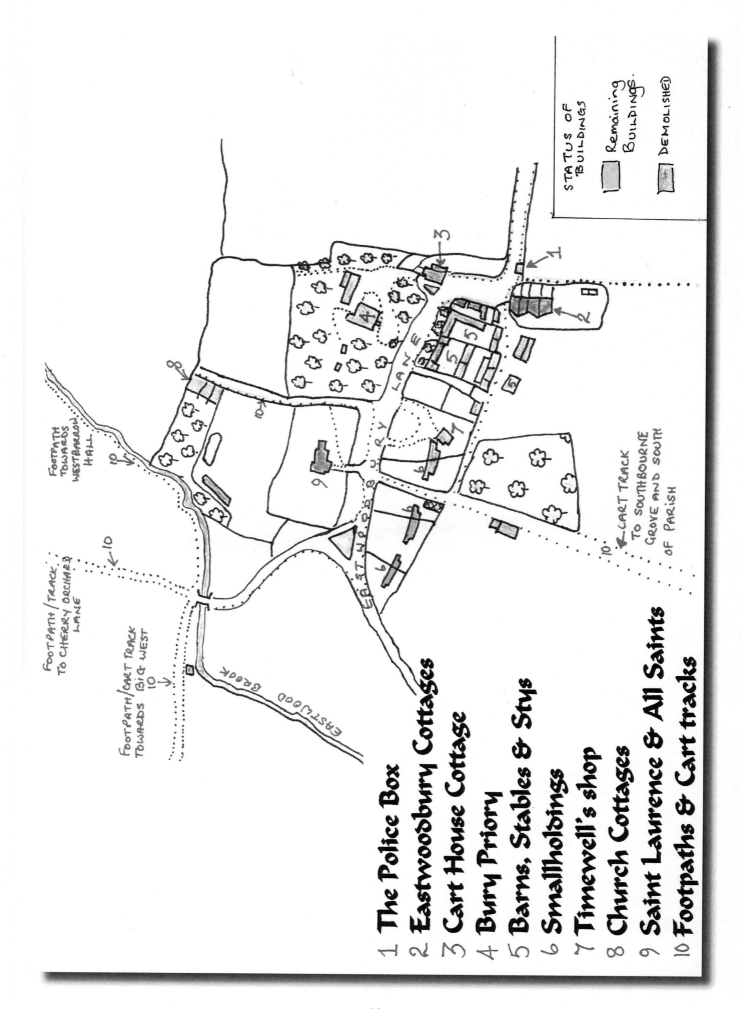

1 The Police Box
2 Eastwoodbury Cottages
3 Cart House Cottage
4 Bury Priory
5 Barns, Stables & Stys
6 Smallholdings
7 Timewell's shop
8 Church Cottages
9 Saint Laurence & All Saints
10 Footpaths & Cart tracks

STATUS OF BUILDINGS

Remaining Buildings.

Demolished

FOOTPATH TOWARDS WESTBROOM HALL

FOOTPATH/TRACK TO CHERRY ORCHARD LANE

FOOTPATH/CART TRACK TOWARDS BIG WEST

EASTWOOD Brook

CART TRACK TO SOUTHBOURNE GROVE AND SOUTH OF PARISH

The vicarage garden

The vicarage stood on a large parcel of land that consisted of lawns to front and rear, rich with numerous fruit trees; idyllic for a Church garden party and fetes festooned with patriotic linen bunting, gently fluttering in welcomed waves of a cool summer breeze tinted with the smell of the damp, off-white canvas tea-tent, housing many a cake, tart and scone franticly baked the night before; and there the tinkling sound of twisted, battered spoon on cheap, chipped china, sporadically drowned by the crinkling, crackling noises emitted from grey, metal, horn-shaped loud-speakers, precariously attached to trees, by an over-zealous middle-aged scout master in baggy knee-length khaki flannel shorts.

From the first aid tent, with white knuckled fingers crossed, he now surveys his reaffixed handiwork as the first tentative parched notes are heard blown through laboriously polished instruments in preparation for yet another selfish rendering of Colonel Bogey; while children smugly grin at one another in the firm belief that they, and only they, are the ones who know certain details of the deceased Adolf Hitler and Heinrich Himmler's anatomy.

Flower, butterfly and bird imprinted crepe summer frocks in shades of pale pink, blue and lilac dress the provincial country scene as rolled-shirt- sleeved fathers, desperate to impress their young fledgling offspring, make flushed giddy fools of themselves at the stained, sacking-backed coconut shy.

From the rear of the house, inner town dwellers stare, transfixed in envious awe at the extended view of vast lush open countryside across to Cherry Orchard then northwest to Nobles Green and beyond.

Among such visitors perhaps, were those who in future years passed the plans to engulf in drab brick, steel and concrete, all the natural beauty they had one so enthusiastically praised.

Extract from 'No Skeletons' (copyright 2001 – Peter Monk)

Upper Edward Hall Farm

Horse racing

Eastwood Dramatic Society

Southend Council

Southend Football Team

Borough Coach Services

Bell Hotel

Stanway Coaches

Upper Edwards Hall Farm, Eastwood was the home of the mayor and mayoress of Southend-on-sea, as after 20 years of public service, Alderman H.H. Smith, JP had been chosen as Mayor of the Borough and his wife, Eileen, the mayoress.

The Southend Standard at the time was probably the first to use a term which is today far from complimentary, when they described the Mayor as a true Essex boy. However, they were describing him as someone who had lived in the county from his childhood and in this area since 1918, someone who had the area in his heart.

'Revd, Woolcott, Eileen Smith, H H Smith and Margaret Woolcott'.

A man of varied interests, Alderman Smith loved sports, and the sport of football was high on his list. He played and officiated at amateur football and was an executive at Chelmsford FC. Southend United elected him as Chairman in 1954, after a period as a director. Talking to local schoolboys, he asked them to keep up playing football when they left school, as the sport would help them in life.

Another abiding passion was horses and Alderman Smith was a well-known racehorse owner and breeder of horses; he was one of only a few people in this part of the county to hold a licence under Jockey Club rules for both flat racing and jumping. On the day he was invested with his chain of office, both the mayor and his son, Henry, were suffering from injuries related to their love of horses.

During his youth, Alderman Smith was a member of Eastwood Dramatic Society, and this was where he met his wife-to-be, Eileen Weston. Eileen had always taken a prominent part in village and community affairs. She was a well-known singer and a leading lady in the local operatic society, as well as being a leading member of Eastwood Wine Circle. She was described as being a quiet, gentle and friendly lady of great personal charm.

Garter Blue

Both of them took part in the shows put on at Eastwood Memorial Hall. They married in 1926, living at first in North Road, Southend, and then at 53, Boston Avenue. Their daughter, Joy, was born in 1927 and their son, Henry in 1930.

In his earliest years, Bert's (as he was known) father had an off-licence in Commercial Road, East. The family, which now included Arthur, Bert's younger brother, moved to the Cauliflower Public House in Rainham and attended Palmer's College, Grays.

During the First World War, at the age of 16, he drove a taxi taking army officers into London. The family moved to Southend after the War. Bert borrowed from his father to purchase a tipper lorry with solid tyres, and soon after, a second lorry.

Weston's Stores

The business had moved on into coaches and then buses. With his brother-in-law, Reg Spray and others, they started Borough Services, which ran between Southend and Grays. They also operated local routes. In those days, bus operators were chasing one another for fare-paying customers. In 1934, he sold the bus station in London Road, Southend, to the Eastern National Bus Company.

That same year, he took over the licence of The Spread Eagle public house in Prittlewell. He became a councillor for Southend Council, standing firstly as independent, but later joined the Conservatives.

About this time, he became a director of Southend United Football Club, and later, in 1952, became chairman. He was the prime mover in taking Southend United Football Club to a ground of their own at Roots

Smith Haulage in Southend

Hall. During this time, he had a building business and his foreman on the sites was Sid Broomfield, and he moved to Roots Hall to become site foreman, much to the chagrin of son, Henry, who said they had lost their best man. This period is documented in the local paper of that time, the Southend Standard.

In 1935, the licence of The Bell Hotel, Leigh, was transferred by H.H. Smith to the new public house built by Taylor Walker breweries. The new Bell Hotel opened in 1936, and the family lived there for the first year before moving to 98, Boston Avenue. During this time, he was building the shops and flats adjacent to The Bell, also houses and bungalows to the rear of the hotel. The shops were designed for specific trades. There was a fish shop, a grocer's, a greengrocer's, a butcher's and a newsagent's. This development was part of the Bentall's Estate. Semi-detached houses were priced at £500 and semi-detached bungalows were £350. There was also a petrol station with flats above.

In 1937, he bought Lovedeans farm, Hockley, and Kingsman's Farm, Hullbridge, and started building a new house at Lovedeans. This farm overlooked the River Crouch, but the land is very heavy. Cows were purchased and the Lovedeans' Friesian herd was formed and milking machines were installed. The family moved in 1938 into the new house.

After the outbreak of War, for financial reasons, the farms had to be sold. The tenancy of Flemmings Farm, Eastwood, was taken at this time. It was owned by Mr Sparrow, the vet of Rochford (known as The Horse Doctor). All machinery and livestock etc. were driven to Flemmings. The cows were driven along the roads and through Gusted Hall Lane and then along the track through the woods. At this time, Flemmings Farmhouse cottages had no mains water or electricity.

In 1941, the War Agricultural Committee requested that the farm became joined with the adjoining Upper Edwards Hall Farm. This had been owned by the Bridge family and included the land, the farmyard and the bungalow known as 'Lichfield', standing in line with Green Lane. This was overgrown with a mass of hawthorn and blackthorn bushes, etc., all of which had to be cleared. This was achieved with a Standard Fordson tractor and chain and all ploughed with a single-furrow plough. He was also asked to farm the field at Rochford Corner, where the row of shops now stands. A lease-lend tractor was assigned to the farm, a Mineapolis Moline.

Much of this cleared area became Edwards Hall Park, with the horse ride which was part of the racehorses' gallop area. The south side of the park is the Edwards Hall Estate with Edwards Hall School and playing field, St David's Church and the adjacent shops on the Rayleigh Road, Eastwood.

Between Green Lane and Flemmings Lane was an isolation field which was purchased by HH Smith from Rochford Council. The Isolation Hospital was demolished and a main water supply was taken from this field to Flemmings Farm which had no main water supply at that time. On this field today stands a bungalow and a barn that was owned by Harland Tyres.

The Pest House or Isolation Hospital. This one was built in 1904 a cost of £149. One stood on Green Lane and another on the south side of Prince Avenue on Bentall's land, opposite Brendon Way

HH joined the Home Guard as a lieutenant, was in charge of transport for the Southend area, his own transport being a motor bike. A milk round was started, known as Upper Edwards Hall Dairies, supplying Eastwood and parts of Rayleigh. Rationing was in force by this time. The transport was pony milk-floats.

In 1943 they moved into Tudor Lodge, near to Tudor Road. In 1948, they bought Upper Edwards Hall Farmhouse and farmyard, remaining as tenant of the farm land.

Other businesses were Stanway Coaches, Ltd, Stanway Contracts, Ltd, the latter being the building and gravel pit firm. The pits were at Rochford and Woodham Walter, and his tipper lorries supplied sand and gravel around the district.

Another enterprise was owning and training racehorses. Fortunately, one of these, Garter Blue, won 11 races on the flat and National Hunt. Bert became Mayor of Southend for 1956/7, a year he and his wife thoroughly enjoyed. And in 1958, when his son, Henry, married, he and his wife moved to Clifftown Parade.

After his death in 1961, Upper Edwards Hall was sold and demolished by the builders who bought it. Gravel Road was extended and runs through what was part of the front garden. The old house stood in what is now Tudor Close. The old farmyard has bungalows built on it. H.H. (Bert), and Eileen, who survived him by 34 years, are buried in Eastwood churchyard.

H. H. Smith (written by Henry Smith, his son)

Tudor Road

Jones' corner

Springwater Road

Population

Deliveries

I was always wandering off and I was often threatened with terrible things if I ever left the gateway. But on one occasion, on a scorching hot day in around 1949, Carol Sullivan said that we should meet my Mum and help her back with the shopping. Bored with playing dust pictures, I agreed. We went down Tudor Road to Jones Corner. I had shorts on. I was so burned by the time that we had found out that Mother had walked to Eastwood Rise that I had to be carried home and put to bed with severe sun stroke. I was very ill and Mother had been frantic with worry when she returned home to find no-one waiting at the gate.

Eileen Speight's parents marry at St Laurence.

Alderman HH Smith was Mayor; he had an Alsatian which used to fight with Mac, a Scottie dog. The Alsatian was remembered by Alan Totham because when the doorstep was being cemented on their bungalow in Springwater Road, the dog left its paw print in the wet cement. Mr Smith also had a lovely racehorse called Garter Blue.

In 1953 there was a dog called Paddy, a mongrel, who had an Irish temperament, no doubt following his name. He could follow a cyclist for miles, snapping at their feet and wheels. The grocer's boy on his bike rode along Springwater Road at his peril! And any stray cat or dog venturing out into the rutted roadway suffered the same fate.

John and David Smee owned Paddy and loved him dearly. One day Paddy snapped at something that he lived to regret to the end of his days. He saw something move over by the bomb hole and made a grab for it; it was an adder. One quick bite and is sank its fangs into Paddy and the battle was over. Paddy lay on the ground yelping and howling while the adder slithered away. Paddy was very ill; his neck swelled to a colossal size and he could hardly move, let alone eat or drink. But Paddy pulled through; his neck went quite flabby and the loose skin would flap around. He was cured of chasing snakes or cats across the bomb site, but could never quite resist chasing the grocer's boy on the bike.

Jones' corner

People who lived and worked in Eastwood 1930 onwards were :-

Eileen	15 Benvenue Avenue (still there)
Ann Daniels	Jones Corner
Ann Webb	Opp Eastwood Park
Valerie Bacon	Nobles Green
Betty Heathcote	Arterial Road
Gladys Trimm	Eastwood Road
Helen Jones	Glenwood Avenue
Peter/Paul Braybrook	Glenwood Avenue
Madeleine Southwold	Glenwood Avenue
Panda Moore	Dandies Drive
The Bells	Tudor Road
The Johnsons	Tudor Road
Auntie Pinkie	Eastwood Rise
George and Mary Harris	Eastwood Rise
Bush	Owned gravel business, Gravel Road
Clysts Nurseries	Jones Corner
Lilliput Garage	
Claydone Coblers	
Daniels Greengrocers	

Lilliput Garage

Wilshens Cycle Shop – owners also of a garage at Jones' Corner
Cornishes Brickfields and Removals

The Roots	Gravel Road
Mrs Fisher	Springwater Road
Mr and Mrs Totham	Springwater Road
Harts	Coal Merchants
Mr Fennel	Springwater Road (an army colonel and JP – played Father Christmas at Eastwood Junior School
Mr Jolly	Springwater and Eastwood Rise (was a farmer and sold off land in the early 1960's)

Bibby, Trussler, Manser, Buckley, Smee, Allen, Cousins, Capps, Moor, Draper were all local names.
Red buses left Jones Corner to go to Leigh
Bread was delivered by horse and cart – Howards Dairies delivered by float.
A van delivered fish once a week
Where The Oakwood stands now, there was a wooden mission-type hut, for a men-only club.
A wooden bridge was used to cross the stream in Bygrave Road.
There was a pig farm opposite the bomb site in Springwater.

The following people lived in Springwater Road:-
The Ardleys, The Garwoods, The Fennells, Mrs Fisher, The Sullivans, The
Hills, The Speights, Harold Down, The Thornes, The Locks, The Peters,
The Johnsons, The Hales and The Kingstons.

Val Speight

Sutton Road

Three Ashes Farm

Boat building

I was living at "Sunnyholme" 29, Rochefort Drive, Rochford from 1934 until 1958 when I was married. Eastwood St Laurence was our parish church at that time.

The Three Ashes Inn was on the south side of Sutton Road, about 60 yards further down the road from the Anne Boleyn. It was pulled down by a Mr Bridge and in its place was a yard, with some lock-up garages. In front of the lock-up garages were two First World War army huts, known as Woodbine Villas. My grandfather, H.T. Theobald, Senior, hired the yard from Mr Bridge from about 1945 until he died in 1955. He was a boat builder; aided at various times by his grandsons, Peter and I, he built clinker-built dinghies and did boat repairs for other people. He also did general house carpentry, repairs and woodwork.

Grandfather was employed to do some of the roof work for houses on Bentall's Estate, and my father painted and decorated pairs of semi-detached bungalows there, both inside and out, for the princely sum of £15.00 for the pair'

Derek Theobald

H.T. Theobald in the Three Ashes Inn Yard, boat building in 1949

Leighfields Road

Eastwood School

The woods

The gypsies

My mother managed to borrow some money from her mother to put down a deposit on a bungalow at 56, Leighfields Road, Eastwood, and as that was the same time that I was due to start school, my brother John and I started together. We would walk to the bottom of Leighfields Road with 2 pennies in our possession, and get a bus round to the school for one of the pennies. My brother taught me to go upstairs and lie down on the seat so that when the conductor came upstairs to take the fares, he would see no legs or feet, and think that he had been mistaken about seeing two little children go up there. When we got to the school the idea was to jump off the bus before he caught you. That would give us a penny to spend on sweeties at the shop next door to the school. And what a lot you could get for a penny in those far-off days. The farthing was still legal tender – a quarter of a penny, so you could buy four black jacks or fruit salads for the penny, or even better, two everlasting gobstoppers! They seemed to last for hours and we would keep taking them out of our mouths to see what colour the new layer was! Such simple pleasures! It was possible to walk home, although it seemed a long way when I was only five years old, but it would give us another penny saved.

My first schoolroom was the original Victorian Eastwood school room and the infants used it in 1950. There must have been about forty of us in the class, and the teacher was the kindest and firmest lady I had ever met. We had little bottles of milk given us each day; they held a third of a pint, and during the cold weather, the crates of bottles would stand out in the yard, getting frozen so that the milk would expand and all the tops would be pushed off the bottles by the ice! The schoolroom had a large round coal boiler in one corner and round it was an enormous fire guard to protect us from the ferocity of the heat generated at close quarters. On rainy days, all our coats would be loaded on to the fire guard to dry them before playtime, and the room would be full of the smell and steam from forty little coats and the smoky residue of the fire.

Munns Corner now Rochford Corner

The teacher's desk was on a wooden plinth, so that when she was seated she could make sure that every one was at work. But although we did work hard, it was not unpleasant; misdemeanours were dealt with swiftly, and by today's standards, brutally. The headmaster, Mr Heppel, would use the slipper on the bad boy's behinds and the bad girls had to suffer the humiliation of standing in the corner until they could be nicer! I really do not believe that any long-term harm came to any child from this treatment; it was no worse than the behaviour of any other of Creation's creatures to its offspring.

The dinner hall at the school was for both infants and juniors and the older children would bring the dinners to the tables for the younger ones. There were eight of us to each table, and we had to say a prayer before the food was served;

> Thank you for the world so sweet
> Thank you for the food we eat
> Thank you for the birds that sing
> Thank you, God, for everything
> Amen

Often it was sung to a simple tune and it sounded really nice in the arched canteen, whose former use had been as an air-raid shelter! It was made of corrugated iron, and was a complete curved structure which was pulled down just a few years later as improvements were made to the school buildings.

We little ones used to sit at our tables and wait for the older children to bring us our dinners. Sometimes there would be a crash as a plate hit the floor but usually all went well, until the day when the monitors brought only seven dinners to my table and I didn't get one!! I remember screaming the place down and my brother, who was a monitor, rushing over to my table to see what was the matter with me! I must have blamed him as he was on duty that day.

When I moved into the second class, we were schooled in a building at the back of the school, nearer to the park, and it had a wooden veranda at the front. I expect the class room was a bit crowded, because we used to compete to be the ones sent out on to the veranda with easels and paints – it was the most wonderful free feeling that I have never forgotten!

I think it was during Coronation Year that we had an eclipse and we were all warned about the dangers of looking at the sun without some sort of protection to our eyes. Some children brought in the negatives from their camera films and others brought in sunglasses, but one secret that our teacher taught us was that

The Congregational Church Outing

61

you could see a reflection in a still bowl of water. So we all provided ourselves with some sort of container, and one wag bunged up the plughole under the playground water fountain for those who didn't have a container. I remember staring, spellbound, into the bowl and watching the miracle happen before my very eyes! The negative of the movement and the shadow cast beneath.

There was also a pageant to celebrate the Coronation and my mother made John a wonderful costume so that he could be Walter Raleigh for the day!

The actual Crowning Ceremony was the first to ever be broadcast on TV, but in those days there was only one TV in the whole road as far as I know. Mrs Downs invited in as many people as she could fit into her front room. Being so little, I had a place at the front and looked up to the set which seemed very high and very, very small! The picture was in black and white, but to me seeing all those princesses in their beautiful frocks was the main thing – it was probably the first time I had ever seen TV!

There are some tiny photos in my collection of John and I holding our cat – she was a beautiful tortoiseshell and she had two lots of kittens, each time a ginger and a black. The ginger survived in one litter and the black survived in the other, but when we moved away, I have no idea what happened to the cat.

The road was unmade when we moved to Eastwood and after some time, they put down concrete. I drew my initials in the concrete, and was quite disappointed when I came back several years later to find that they were not there.

Even when the road was unmade, though, everything one wanted could be delivered. The coal and the milk were delivered by horse and cart. The bread came in a handcart and fish and eggs and ice cream were also brought to the door – it was a real luxury.

There was a set of shops in Eastwood when I was little, as well as having things delivered. There was a general store which it seemed sold everything. There were bottles full of all sorts of sweets; cheese and butter which had to be cut according to how much the customer wanted; tea which had to be weighed. They sold paraffin and soap, some of which was household soap for washing and some for toiletry, but little of it was wrapped. There were no plastic bags; we had to take our own baskets to the shop to bring stuff home.

There was a wet-fish shop where my red-headed friend Ruth lived. She always had warts on her hands and my Mum said it was because she used to play with her egg-shells. I've not heard this theory from anywhere else, so I really don't know where the idea came from! We used to go to Sunday school together, Ruth and I, and I have a photo of us taken at Maldon on a Sunday school outing, with our dresses tucked into our knickers, just before one of us got pushed into the water – I think it was her!

When I came home from school, I had to fish for the key inside the letter box where it was held on a piece of string; we were the 'latch-key kids' who had to amuse themselves till Mum came home from work, and I have to say I am sure we got up to all sorts of mischief during that time!

Mrs Downs lived further down the road and she had three or four strapping sons, although she was only a tiny little sparrow of a woman herself. We were told that we were to go to her if we needed anything, but apart from that we pleased ourselves. We would get on our bikes and cycle across to Progress Road, where construction on the road itself was almost complete, and one or two factories were already in production. There was one factory which must have been making glass egg timers, because I remember poring through piles of broken ones that had been cast out in the in hopes of finding one that worked – I often did, but I am sure Mum would have had a fit if she had seen where I had found them.

Once Mrs Downs wanted to clean out the fish pond in her garden and we said we would look after the fish so we put them in a bucket and took them back for a swim in the bath – Mum wasn't too pleased about that one!

John and some of the older boys had worn a dirt track from their bikes where they used to compete in stunts and races; I think there may have been one or two small motorbikes there as well but I am not sure about that. Nothing would surprise me as the boys of Eastwood seemed a rough and tough lot to me as I was growing up! I had to go with my brother to all sorts of places as there was nothing else to do and I think he must have promised Mum that he would look after me! I know it was onerous at times, and we did fall out from time to time; it must have been very difficult for him having a kid sister hanging around in all his free time.

At the bottom of our garden was a large meadow, and at the top of the road the woods began, so there was really never any shortage of safe places to play. One of the Dads had rigged a rope over the limb of an oak tree, and I can still picture the worn groove below where our feet swung to and fro. Once, when I was off to the woods, I was frightened by a man carrying a cocked gun over his arm; I expect he was only looking for a rabbit for the pot, but I didn't know that – I thought of Mother telling me

> My mother said I never should
> Play with the gypsies in the wood
> If I did, she would say
> Naughty girl to disobey!

Peter and Jean Theobald married at St Laurence in March 1955

She was always aware that Eastwood was full of gypsies, but there was nothing she could do about that, and there were a lot attending school spasmodically that she didn't know about, but they tended not to mix with the regular children, anyway.

There were good times, though; there was no cinema in Eastwood of course, but we were often allowed to go to 'the pictures' in Rayleigh or Southend or Leigh. There were Saturday morning picture clubs at most of the cinemas and if one got boring or too riotous we would go to another. There would be a feature film, one of those now described as a 'B' movie, a cartoon or Laurel and Hardy, and a serial like Buck Rogers, with a cliff-hanger to make you want to come back the following week.

Once I remember going to the Rayleigh pictures, that was The Regal near Rayleigh Mount, and we saw a pineapple on the greengrocer's stall for sixpence, which was about the amount of spare money we had. We smuggled it into the pictures and one of the boys cut it up into chunks in the dark, with his penknife. We were very sticky and late coming home that day, so I think we may have spent the fare on the pineapple and had to walk home!

Kiti Theobald

Springwater Road

I grew up at 19, Springwater Road. I remember Beryl and her father, Mr   Podger, the builder, well. Also Mr H Smith, the builder of our house. The house was built on the place just north of where a bomb had made a huge crater. He had a large Alsatian dog that my friends and I used to ride on. The dog left its paw print in the wet cement on our doorstep – I imagine it is still there!

I lived in the area between 1955 and 1980, and attended Eastwood Primary School (for a time in the Victorian building) and later Edwards Hall and Eastwood High School for Boys.

I remember dating a girl called Sheila Potter who lived in Woodside about 1966!

Alan Totham

Granny Gooch

Gypsy folklore

Elim Chapel

Eastwood Rise

The brock works

Baptist Chapel

Mr Joy, the Chemist

The Fire Service

ABOVE: Eastwood Rise in the 1920s, almost unrecognisable to residents of the area today

ABOVE: A typical Eastwood home long before the area was swallowed up by Southend and Rochford

RIGHT: A snap from reader Bill Caten's family album. Bill is pictured on the left

Offered to Charlie Grimwade in 1930's for £100 Dagmar Sandhill Road

I lived in Eastwood from 1922 until 1939, firstly in Nore Road in a bungalow, then in a house in Eastwood Road opposite Ned Ford's blacksmiths. I was born in Dulwich, London and was aged 9 when we moved here.

I knew the old midwife Granny Gooch who lived near the Gypsy field opposite the rise. (I was only about 10 at the time so over the years I thought that she would live forever.) The Gypsies would not consider having anyone else to deliver their babies except Granny Gooch. This was at a time when if the last of a line of the family died, the body was placed in their own caravan, then a funeral pyre was made of it. They were always fighting and the winner of the fight would hold the loser down, whip out a pointed knife or dagger, then prick his opponent's earlobes until the blood ran, just to prove he was the victor.

A small Catholic corrugated iron chapel stood on the on the corner of Nore Road, at the edge of the Gypsy Field. This was approached by negotiating an open bridge made of old railway sleepers, which spanned the local brook, whose source is at Rayleigh Weir. In those days it was not piped anywhere but was open along its whole length. A regular party of people who came from the Elim chapel in Rayleigh would hold services there for the Gypsy congregation. A young lady member would accompany them on an American pedal organ. This young lady had a good soprano voice, and was in big demand by the Gypsy Grandmas, to go round to their caravans to sing hymns for them. She would look at the houses on the opposite side of the road and wonder who lived there, little knowing that one day the man that she would marry would live there. He, on the other hand, had no idea of what went on in the Chapel. Years afterwards a song was written called "In the Chapel in the Moonlight" which still brings back those memories after sixty years of marriage between Muriel and me.

One November the 5th a gang of us boys, led by the local Drover's son, who was about 25 years old, named Sonny Jollye, pulled an old car chassis, complete with tireless, rimless wheels, to the top of Eastwood Rise, then all jumped on and away we went, belting down the slope towards the Main Road. Needless to say we all jumped off before the bottom, leaving our nondescript mode of transport to carry on across the road and through the fence of the house opposite.

Further along "The Rise" there used to be a breaker's yard belonging to an old man who bought and sold old car parts and tyres. There were several stacks of these tyres about ten or twelve high in his yard, so before the night was out somebody thought that as the fireworks had all been used up the next best thing would be to set light to the tyres. Thus we had not only an enormous bonfire, but also the added thrill of watching the local fire brigade put it out! Beckwith's lorry yard was also near the top of 'The Rise' next to a bungalow. (shown 3rd left on the photo)

Eastwood Rise when it was an unmade road

At the top of Eastwood Rise, there was a brickfield which produced red bricks and "The Rise" itself started as a cart track leading to it. This was continually being made up with broken red brick rubble, so that for years it was known as the "Red Road" long before it was called Eastwood Rise. In wet weather, the red mud was just another inconvenience our Mothers had to put up with. This brickfield had been worked out some years before I arrived on the scene, and the resulting quarry hole had filled with water, which was soon stocked with fish for the keen Anglers who frequented its banks. As far as I am aware this lake is still there! This became known as New England Pond and was part of Flemings Farm.

When about ten, I was introduced to the Baptist Chapel at the bottom of Nobles Green where I joined the Sunday School where I was known for placing drawing pins on the teachers chairs and breaking windows (by accident) with balls. After a while I tamed down by perseverance of the teachers and was opted into the Life Boys a similar organisation to the Cubs. Chrissie Walker, the butcher's daughter was our Mistress at the time.

Then, as I grew older, I transferred to the "Boys Brigade". I was proud of my polished belt, buckle and pillbox hat on the side of my head and looked forward to drilling and marching. Eventually I became a side drummer in their drum, fife and bugle band, We enjoyed marching up to the Rayleigh Baptist chapel along Eastwood Road, playing marching tunes for all we were worth. The two officers in charge of us were the two Cornish brothers, Charlie and Cyril, sons of the owner of the well known Cornish brickworks.

Beckwith's yard was in Eastwood Rise

I left school at fourteen years old and was put to work at the Cornish Brickfield and those hard, red, bricks were known and sought after all over the country. I was given a job on the brick making machine which used moulds to make three bricks at a time. Each mould weighed about twenty pounds empty. I stood in front of a box of sharp sand, scooped sand into a mould, emptied it out, then slid it into the side of the machine, which then proceeded to ram brick clay into it, (the sand in the mould was to stop the clay from sticking to it).

At my tender age, working from 6am till 6pm with only a ten minute break morning and afternoon, and half an hour midday for dinner break, I was just about exhausted by the end of the day, especially as I had to traipse back home across three fields.

During the Second World War, I was taken Prisoner of War by the Japanese (1942) and slaved on the Death Railway for three and a half years. I put my survival down to my early upbringing, being breast fed, eating good country food and a tough start at work as the reason I survived at all. The wood at the rear of Eastwood Rise was a good training ground for the jungle also. My mates would dare me to run through the woods in the middle of the night, I managed this by climbing from my bedroom window, so that my parents never knew.

My initiation also included bathing in the nude. This started off when the sewer bed was being dug out in the fields at the ends of Connaught and York roads when I was about eleven or twelve. Us boys would watch the great digging machines loading the light railway trucks which ran on the narrow gauge lines right back to the main Eastwood Road where the spoil was scooped into lorries.

After a few weeks, two enormous holes were evident. These had sloping sides so rainwater flooded in, forming two lakes about two feet deep. Of course this was too much temptation for us, so in the warm summer weather we stripped off and swam about in it, completely ignoring the fact that we ended up covered in mud, our clothes included, as we put them on again, causing another headache for our long suffering mothers.

Another exciting pastime we got up to while the workmen were away at week-ends included the railway. We would pull the light trucks to the top of the slope about three hundred yards away, then get on and ride down again over a brook and round a sharp bend. The trouble started when some idiot, who hadn't been included in our gang, decided to get his own back by placing a large log across the track just round the bends, so it was invisible until we were right on top of it. Of course we all went flying. Then one of my mates told me that my face was bleeding, caused by a branch sticking out, so I got my handkerchief to staunch the blood. I managed to hide this from my Mother until the next day, and then she sent me along to our local chemist Mr Joy, whose shop was at Jones Corner. Mr Joy was as good as a Doctor and as there were no Doctors in the area most people would go to see Mr Joy with their ailments. He sat me on a chair, saying "you should have come yesterday!" gave me some Sal Volatile to counteract any feeling of sickness, then proceeded to sew the wound together with two stitches, then sent me away without charging anything. What Chemist would do this today?

A footpath used to run from the top of Eastwood Rise across several fields, past the top of Nobles Green and end up at the two farms farther along. A corrugated iron building has been built alongside this path, now called Green Lane; with a barbed wire fence ten feet high, with an overhang of two feet on the inside at the top and it was some time before we found out it was an Isolation Hospital for Smallpox patients. I used to travel; along this path from home on my way to my Uncles market garden which stretched from Nobles Green to Dandies Drive at the top. In fact his dog Dandy was called after Dandies Drive. My Uncles name was Harry Scraggs, he and my Aunt Nell were well known around there at this time, when they would sell their vegetables and fruit. I used to look forward to travelling to Rochford Market by cart, drawn by "Prince" the horse, going across Warners Railway Bridge on the way.

After the War I rejoined the Fire Service at Rayleigh. While there, we were often called to Eastwood, on one occasion to the afore-mentioned sewage works, where a large square space of ground was enclosed by earth banks about three feet high. These were to hold the liquid sludge, which was then allowed to dry off in the open air. On arrival we saw that the grass had caught fire so proceeded to make our way around to the outbreak along the top of the earth banks. One of our number whose trade was as a milkman (We were also called "Part Time" although invariably we were called out to more fires than the Full timers" who had official time off) decided to take a short cut across one of the sludge areas, thinking it was dry, whereas it only had a crust about an inch thick, so he sank into the foul smelling gunge up to his knees. We put the fire out, and then went back to the appliance, including Eric the Milkman, but we wouldn't let him get on, and made him run behind for some distance before hosing him down to get all the residue off.

Another time, there was a fire call to a Nudist Colony situated in the fields at the top of Clarence Road. On the way the officer in charge told us with a straight face, "Now, don't forget, when we arrive, strip off and go in wearing helmets, axe and boots only!" Needless to say that when we arrived we found it was a hoax call, much to our disappointment.

Eastwood Football Club - 1950's

Dick Wilkins

(Dick Wilkins lived opposite Ned Ford's yard in a semi-detached bungalow. He was a painter and decorator, a fact that was advertised by a sign on the flank wall- Ed.)

This last section of a rather long chapter commemorates those who are remembered as living in Eastwood, but who have already passed on at the time of writing:-

Granny Gooch – This lady was a midwife, especially to many of the travelling families, many of whom would not consider having a confinement without Granny in attendance.

Mr Joy the chemist – Mr Joy had a shop at Jones Corner, where medicine was dispensed, together with a great deal of common sense advice. He would wherever possible treat those who came to him without sending them to hospital. He had a neat style of stitching, too. A much loved person, who cared a great deal for the people of Eastwood.

Mr Stedman – the school caretaker during the 1940's at Eastwood School. He lived in the School House at the front of the buildings with his family who also attended the school. The rule of not running or sliding in the corridors was sacred and never attempted in Mr Steadman's presence.

Rose Nunn – mostly known as the caretaker of Eastwood Church. A local girl, who had an interest in all that was going on in the whole of Eastwood. Rose knew everyone, and everyone knew her. Not a person to take liberties with, she worked hard and expected everyone to do the same. She lived in Church Cottages.

Jack Overall – Willow Tree Cottage, Eastwoodbury Lane. Worked at Cockethurst Farm for 52 years. Was presented with a gold medal at the Essex Show in July, 1954.

Willow Cottage opposite the Glebe

Geoffrey Sleigh-Johnson – Organist and choirmaster at St Laurence and St David's in the 1960's.

Nurse Powell – Village nurse and midwife in the 1940's. Cycled for miles on her distinctive bike to do her rounds.

Jack Porter – lived at Sunnyside, Whitehouse Lane. Worked at the Fowler Farms and at the Cornish Brickfields, later had his own window cleaning round.

Miss M Rose – History and English teacher at Eastwood High School and first Headmistress of Eastwood Girls' School in the 1960's.

Frank Munns – Ingleside, Rochford Road (Whitehouse Road) was the home of the Munns Family and their influence caused this area to be called Munns Corner before it came to be called Rochford Corner. The family were leading lights in the Eastwood Horticultural Society, regularly winning prizes in local shows. When Frank moved out of Eastwood, he called his new home Inglewood too and made it as much like the original as possible.

Albert Keoch - Montrose, Rochford Road (Whitehouse Road) was the home of Mr. Keoch, a Market Gardener, who without doubt grew the best tomatoes in the whole area, in the days before "Cherry Tomatoes", Mr. Koch would put the tiny fruit in a special container where they would be available for next to nothing, but flavour was assured.

Mr and Mrs Timewell - Lived in a smallholding opposite Eastwood Church, where they opened a small general store which even had petrol pumps conveniently placed alongside the road. Later, they opened a bigger shop and Post Office near the entrance to the Airport in Eastwoodbury Crescent.

❑ *More community pictures appear on page 21*

Faithful helpers: Gwen Bambrook, Beryl Brown and Jean Hall, all members of St Laurence's Church in Eastwood, raising funds on the bric-a-brac stall in the church hall
99/7906

Gwen Bambrook, Beryl Brown & Jean Hall

There must be a small mention here for Beryl Brown, self-styled 'chief cook and bottle-washer' in her role as church warden. If the church looks lovely or the events at the church or the church hall need organising, Beryl is sure to be there, working hard to make sure the wheels run smoothly.

Before leaving this chapter, the following is taken from 'A Memorandum of Occurrences' , a journal written by David Ling, of Rochford:-

1878 – March 24th – Deep snowdrifts

1878/9 – severe winter, late summer, cutting grass for hay and green corn in August

1879 – Harvest continued to October, wheat cutting in October

1881 – Jan 18th – very severe snowstorms, wind east/south-east; roads blocked; 20° frost

1881 – midsummer – comet seen north, called 'The Great Southern Comet'

1881 – Oct 14th – terrific gale, great flood water on the causeway

1882 – Oct and Nov- 'The Great Southern Comet' returned, tail leaning to SW

1886 – Mar 16th – severe frost 32° in workshop

1886 – Dec 8th – terrible gale; wind SW; bar 28

1888 – Aug 1st – heavy rain; wind E; water on the causeway; great flood

1889 – Sept 2nd - The Great Thunderstorm; most vivid lightning and heavy rain.
        The dove house at Rochford Hall was set on fire by lightning

1891 – Mar 9/10 – The Great Thunderstorm and blizzard and gale; wind SE backing to NE; deep snow

1893 – Mar 5th to May 17th – no measurable rain

1897 – June 24th – very severe thunderstorm; when the lightning struck
        Mrs Astey's and Mrs Rutherford's houses in the Market Square, the roof was damaged

1900 – The bridge dividing the parishes of Rochford and Eastwood, first erected in 1772, was rebuilt

1903 – June 15th – great rain; flooded surroundings.
        Since the beginning of June to the end of July, 11 inches of rain has fallen

(Nothing much changes then! – Ed)

A LIST OF EASTWOOD FARMS IN THE MID-TWENTIETH CENTURY

1 Eastwoodbury Manor

2 Eastwood Lodge

3 Cockethurst Farm

4 Upper Edwards Hall

5 Lower Edwards Hall

6 Victoria Farm

7 Flemings Farm

7a. New England Farm

8 Blatches

9 Cherry Orchard

10 West Barrow

11 Wilderness Farm

12 Three Ashes

12a. Purdey's Farm

13 Harp House Farm

14 White's Farm

15 Feeches Farm

16 White House Farm

17 Big West Farm

18 Dandies Farm

19 Hill Farm

20 Barker's Farm

21 Coleman's Farm

22 Highlands Farm

23 Brickhouse Farm

24 Pickett's Farm

25 Little Pickett's Farm

26 Wood Farm

27 Bell House Farm

28 Belfairs Farm

29 Priory Farm

29a. Earl's Hall Manor Farm

30 Rochford Hall

Eastwood produce sold at Rochford Market - Christmas 1928

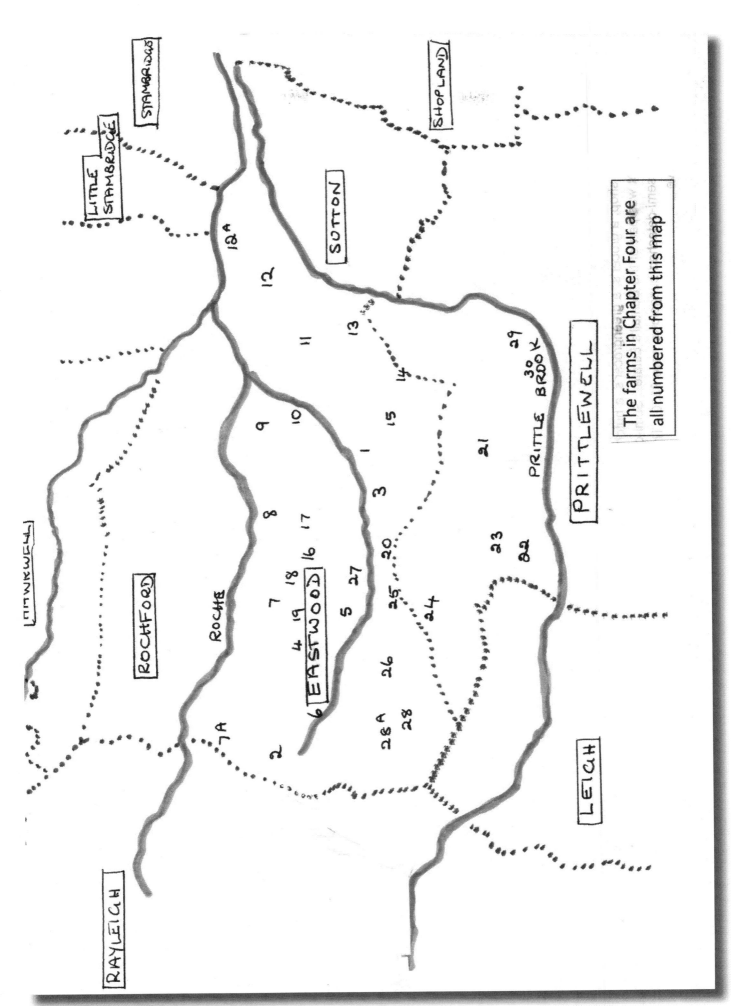

The farms in Chapter Four are
all numbered from this map

RAYLEIGH

STAMBRIDGE

LITTLE STAMBRIDGE

HAWKWELL

ROCHFORD

ROCHF

EASTWOOD

SUTTON

SHOPLAND

PRITTLEWELL

PRITTLE BROOK

LEIGH

18A

12

11

13

14

29

30

10

9

15

21

1

8

16 17

3

23

22

7 18 19

5 27

20

25

24

26

4

28A 28

2

7A

Owners of the Manor of Eastwood

1042 – During the reign of Edward the Confessor, the Lordship belonged to ROBERT de ESSEX, **son of** WIMARC.

1066 – SUENE, **son of Robert. The estate was forfeited to the Crown by** HENRY de ESSEX, **Suene's grandson.**

1204 – HENRY II

1210 – ROBERT de ESTWOOD

1226 – HUBERT de BURGH, Earl of Kent, **by grant of Henry III, then his widow,** MARGARET, Countess of Kent

1260 – JOHN de BURGH

1274 – granted to EDWARD I

1340 – WILLIAM de BOHUN, Earl of Northampton, **by grant of Edward III**

1360 – HUMPHREY de BOHUN. **For lack of a male heir, reverted to the Crown**

1380 – ALBERIC de VERE, Earl of Oxford, **by grant of Richard II**

1390 – EDMUND de LANGLEY, Duke of York, **Richard's Uncle**

1415 – EDWARD, Duke of York, **killed at Agincourt; his widow,** PHILLIPPA, **held a one-third share until her death.**

1431 – RICHARD, Duke of York

1535- THOMAS BULLEN, Earl of Wiltshire and Ormond, **and his son,** GEORGE, Lord Rochford, **by grant of Henry VIII**

1551 – RICHARD LORD RICHE **and his descendants, the** EARLS OF WARWICK **- the line then became extinct.**

1673- DANIEL, Earl of Nottingham, **related by marriage to the Warwick heiress, Lady Essex, and sold by him to Robert Bristow and his descendants**

CHAPTER FOUR
FARMS AND FARMING

There were 33 farms in Eastwood within living memory, none of which exist today, as well as a large number of smallholdings owned by Essex County Council which dated from the end of World War One. In this chapter, we will try to bring you as much detail as possible about what the farms and the farming community were like in the Eastwood of the nineteenth and twentieth centuries, as well as providing some of the history of the changes in ownership and usage, particularly during the 20th century, when nearly all farming was wiped out from Eastwood, as Southend became larger and more urbanised. It seems strangely ironic that now, at the beginning of the 21st Century, people are queuing for allotments in the area to grow their own produce in a part of the county that once had the best grade of farming land, which has nearly all been built over.

In 1803, When Arthur Young was Secretary to the Board of Agriculture he made a survey of agriculture in Essex. At that time there were two principal farmers. One was Asser Vassal, who farmed 350 acres of Cockethurst and the other was Major Carr, who held even more land than this. The Major once drained 400 acres, by having trenches dug and laying faggots (bundles of twigs) and straw before replacing the soil. This cost £6 an acre to achieve, a huge investment, but one which was probably vital to food production in heavy Essex clay soil.

Mr Vassal is recorded as having 100 Old Leicester ewes, 100 Lincoln ewes and 100 shearling sheep. His average clip of wool was 8lbs (about 3.5 kilos) in weight, which in 1804 sold for 1/4d (7p) per pound. All the work on the farms was done by men or horses. The Suffolk was the favourite breed of horse locally, and it would take at least two horses, one man and a boy to plough one acre of land each day. The wages of the men employed on the Eastwood land in the early 19th Century were higher then in other places, possible due to the fact that ale did not form part of their wages, a tradition which was common in other places.

Bury Farm Cottages

Bulky goods would often be transported by cart to the Broomhills Wharf, just below Stambridge Mills, for transport by barge to London and other destinations.

1. EASTWOODBURY MANOR (BURY FARM MANOR)

It is thought that in 1811, this manor and its farm were held by William Weld Wren, who later moved to Cockethurst Farm after the death of his wife, Mary. He died in 1849 and the next record of ownership that comes to light is that of the Stallibrass family in 1870; first, John Waylett Stallibrass, and then Allen Stallibrass in 1902.

Eastwoodbury Manor

During World War Two, the manor was used as the Officers' Mess for the aerodrome, RAF Rochford. The farm was managed by Mr Timewell, Of Weir Farm,

Rayleigh, throughout the war. He also managed Lower Edwards Hall and the Fairway heath land, a lot of responsibility for one man. With most men either conscripted or volunteering to be in the army, there was not a lot of choice, and farm work was very hard, since we had to produce as much food within this country as we could, blockades being set up all around the coast to stop shipping from bringing food into the country.

Cart Lodge for Bury Farm

When the officers left the manor to move to the former isolation hospital near Sutton Ford Bridge, which was roomier for them, the building became more and more derelict, squatters moved in and finally the building was demolished to make more room for the runway.

2. EASTWOOD LODGE

South view of Eastwood Lodge

This lodge was one of many used during the days when Eastwood was the most easterly village of 'The Great Forest'. Hadleigh and Thundersley were also within this forest, and in the 13th Century, the kings of England and their courtiers came to the forest to hunt deer, boar and other game. They may also have stayed at Hadleigh Castle when it was still a viable building in which to stay! It is known that Henry VIII hunted here and that his second wife, Anne Boleyn, had connections with Rochford Hall.

The farm, which originally consisted of 200 acres, was used as a children's home during World War Two, and later as old people's accommodation. It had a gatehouse on the north side of Rayleigh Road, opposite Glenwood Avenue.

In 1927, Kelly's Directory listed Charles Weston as a poultry farmer, living at Lower Eastwood Lodge.

Eastwood Lodge, when combined with Edwards Hall, covered an area of 377 acres.

Lower Eastwood Lodge

3. COCKETHURST FARM

There is much more about Cockethurst Farm and its history in Chapter Five, but as far as farming goes, there were 63 acres recorded in 1928, including a farmhouse and two cottages. There is a strong link between earlier owners of the farm and the Mayflower which carried The Pilgrim Fathers to America in the 17th century, a fact celebrated in the west window of the church. The last farmer to live in Cockethurst Farm was Councillor John Fowler, who farmed four farms, including Dandies and Cherry Orchard.

4. UPPER EDWARDS HALL

Situated on the south side of the beautiful Roach valley, its boundary to the west is the Rochford/Rayleigh boundary and to the south, Rayleigh Road, Eastwood. To the north lies Flemings Farm and to the east was the old fever hospital and Flemings Farm Road off Green Lane.

This was a farm of seventy-five acres, its entrance flanked by an avenue of high elms leading to the farmyard which was situated on high ground. It stood east of Bosworth Road, and was farmed by H. H. Smith, along with Flemings Farm. These two farms were used for a variety of purposes; among the crops grown were wheat, barley, oats, potatoes, peas, spring cabbage, rhubarb, kale, mangolds, lucerne and clover ley. There was grass pasture for dairy cows, heifers and pigs.

The barley and oats were kept for farm use, and the wheat sold off to local millers, either Matthews at Battlesbridge, Browns of Rayleigh Mill or Rankins at Stambridge. Matthews and Rankins used Thames barges to transport the corn via the Crouch. Wheat could only be sown in the autumn, up until October or early November after harvesting, ploughing and cultivating the land ready for drilling, but barley and oats could be sown in autumn or in spring. The potato varieties were Majestic, Epicure and Home Guard as well as Once Grown Scotch Seed, varieties which are mostly unheard of today. They were collected from Rayleigh rail station and placed into chitting boxes in the dark and away from the frosts. If they produced a heavy crop, and not achieving a good price, they would be put into clay clamps on dry land, and the clamps were thatched with straw to keep them in good condition until they were sold to the wholesalers; this was either W H West and Sons at Southend Victoria Goods Yard or Essex and Kent Farmers in North Road, Southend.

West Paddock, Edwards Hall - 1959

Vegetables from the farm were sold to Essex and Kent Farmers who also farmed Three Ashes Farm in the name of the Marshall Brothers.

The 25 or so pigs at Edwards Hall Farm were firstly Essex sows, crossed with Large Whites, and later followed by the Landrace breed. They were housed in pigsties and outside units in the paddock to the west of the farmyard between Gravel Road and Sandhill Road. The 'weaners', at 8 weeks old, as well as the sows from who they were taken, were fed on Tottenham pudding, which was food waste that was produced in the Southend area and cooked at the Southend Sewerage Works in Eastern Avenue. It was placed into heavy steel dustbins which could be collected by local farmers for feeding of pork pigs. It was collected for Edwards Hall pigs by the half-ton! They were also fed on boiled chap potatoes. Feed for cattle and pigs was bought from Matthews of Battlesbridge and Browns or Rayleigh Mill.

Upper Edwards Hall has seen several farmers. There was a Mr Scraggs there during World War I, and then around 1923 it was bought by Mr Bridge who also ran a local bus service - his garage was at the bottom of Bosworth Road and it is believed he also built the bungalows in Tudor and Bosworth Roads. A Mr Sparrow farmed it in the 1930's, the next farmer was Mr Wiffen and in1938 Mr G Adlam kept a herd of cows here and had a local milk round doing two and sometimes three rounds a day.

Lower Edwards Hall

There were in fact many small dairy herds around the area, such as Snell's, beside New England Wood, Mrs RickIns at the top of Nobles Green, Dick Durrell at Dawes Heath, J Flack in the Eastwood Road, and Granville House near Ned Ford's blacksmith shop also kept a few cows. Pasteurisation put an end to all these small milkmen.

In the winter of 1939-40 the one and only tap in the cowshed froze and the water had to be carted from the pond in the pond field. Twice a day they had to break the ice, fill the milk churns and take them via the pony and cart to give the cows a drink.

During the Battle of Britain a Spitfire crashed close to the hedge in the Leg of Mutton Field at the bottom of Mr Kemp's garden in Dandies Drive. The hedge was set alight by the crash.

The main entrance to Edwards Hall was from Rayleigh Road, Eastwood, via a gateway in the Road Field. There was a lodge for the farm where the new flats at the bottom of Tudor Road now stand; this was Edwards Hall Cottage. Three large buildings here contained the milk depots for the wholesaler for the Co-op dairies, Mr Madgewick, who lived in the farm house and had a wholesale milk delivery business at the bottom of Tudor Road. Mr Madgewick, who had bought the farm buildings and the house from Mr Bridge, collected milk from some of the local farms, in competition with Howards Dairies. This depot later became the Whalehide factory, then Helbar Engineering. Mr Bridge had built the original buildings to garage his fleet of buses.

Edwards Hall Farm was 260 acres alone, but when combined with Eastwood Lodge was recorded as 377 acres.

Just before the outbreak of war, in 1937, an avenue of high elm trees which stood on the east side of the farmyard was felled by Sadd's of Maldon to be used for timber.

In 1948 the cowshed was converted into racehorse stables which stood until about 1958 when steel posts were erected on the southern boundary of the front fields to mark out land which Mr Bridge sold to Southend Council in 1920. The school and the estate around it were not built until the 1950's.

Henry Smith on a Fordson Tractor 1944

Lichfield, the farm bungalow

Edwards Hall School currently stands on the site of the farmland, which Mr Bridge had retained, along with the farm bungalow, Lichfield, in line with Green Lane, after the sale of the farmhouse. Edwards Hall Park, a swathe of 30 acres including allotments, was gifted by the Bridge Family to Southend Council. Some of the original hedgerows have been retained, including the horse track which was part of the original gallop.

The Edwards Hall land on its south side was lighter land with gravel and sand mixed in, but the land became heavier to the north and north-east. This farm carried 25 Friesian cows, known as the Lovedown Prefects, with heifer followers kept as replacements. Bull calves were sold in Rochford or Chelmsford markets.

Edwards Hall cattle yard - 1960's

From Left to Right:
Norman Grimwade
Johnny Harmsworth
Sid Broomfield
Jack Grimwade

Upper Edwards Hall Farm sale 1963

Edwards Hall School, east of Bosworth Road off Progress Road.
Part of Upper Edwards Hall Farm

Each year stock taking on the farm was undertaken by Offin and Rumsey, based in South Street, Rochford.

The playing field of the school was graded level, but there was a spring in the middle of the field which initially caused many problems, with water gushing down towards the factories on the Rayleigh Road.

The modern church building which is St. David's Eastwood was consecrated in May 1966. The church was built to replace the Mission Church, a Nissan Hut type of building which had been built on to an older barn. The Mission Church had been dedicated in 1949 by the Bishop of Colchester and was ministered by St Laurence Church. As the church grew funds were raised to provide a permanent church and in 1961 St David's was created as an Ecclesiastical District. The Rev Nugent was installed as Priest in Charge, Mr Towler and Mr Horner were the first Church wardens.

A track shown on the tithe map ran from The Three Ashes Farm, near where the Anne Boleyn is today, by Sutton Road, across the current airport to the south of West Barrow Hall, through to Dandies Farm, Hill Farm, Green Lane Isolation Hospital, then by Upper Edwards Hall Farm to Eastwood Lodge. A George III cartwheel penny was found by Sid Broomfield in the ditch by the oak tree near the farm gate which joined Green Lane. This coin could have been thrown by a huntsman to one of the locals to open the gate during an 18th-Century hunting expedition.

The farmhouse was demolished in 1963. It was 400 years old.' The farmyard remained more or less intact until the remains were pulled down and cleared after the Millennium for a new bungalow estate called 'Tudor Mews'

5. LOWER EDWARDS HALL

The census of 1901 and that of 1911 record the farmer as Oscar Wagenitz. Oscar was German-born, but his wife, Ellen had been born in London. They had seven children living in 1911, with the two eldest sons working on the farm. It is possible that the outbreak of war had a serious effect on the occupation of the sons as well as the upkeep of the farm but the 1921 census is not at present available, so there is no current record available to show what happened to the Wagenitz family.

Lower Edwards Hall Farm was on the south side of Rayleigh Road, which is now Progress Road Industrial Estate, and this was farmed during the war by Mr Timewell who also farmed at Rayleigh Weir. It was a 100-acre farm.

Farm work at the beginning of the war was medieval; cows were milked by hand by the light of the hurricane lamps, there was no electricity at Edwards Hall, horses still ploughed the land and corn was still cut with a scythe around the headlands.

Also, all the fields had names, such as The Road Field, The Leg of Mutton Field, Bosworth Field, Tudor Road Field, The Bungalow Field, The Three Acre Field and the Seven Acre Field. Most of the fields at the time were covered in gorse bushes, yellow broom and blackthorn bushes but these fields were all cleared and cultivated by the next farmer, Mr H Smith. Some of the farm buildings were still standing in the 1950's, as Progress Road was being built.

Sand and ballast were dug out of the Tudor Road field for the construction of bungalows in Bosworth and Tudor Roads.

6. VICTORIA FARM

This was a small farm on the east side of Victoria Road, facing Rayleigh Road on the south side, next to the forge belonging to Ned Ford, the blacksmith. Cows were still being kept here in the 1920's. Sometimes known as Granville House, a man named Billy Fisher lived here in the 1920's. On the land to the south was a pumping station.

7. FLEMINGS FARM

Wally Avery and Mary Harris at Flemings Farm

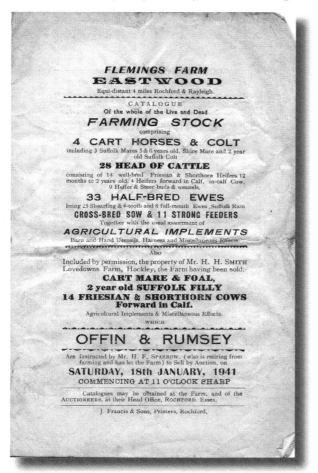

Sale Catalouge

Flemings Farm

Flemings Farm was a typical Essex weatherboarded house that had been very well restored by a Mr and Mrs Turner. The farm originally covered 130 acres, but 100 acres were later transferred to George Taylor. It was bought in 1914 by Pat Sparrow, who also farmed Edwards Hall. At first, the cows were milked by hand, and then a milking machine was brought in. It has also been owned by Harry Sparrow, of the family of Rochford vets, and Bertrand Edward Moss was the farm bailiff at that time.

The farm was rented by H. H. Smith in 1941 on instructions from the War Office. The cow shed was improved with new concrete floor and stalls and a feeding manger for 25 cows. An orchard stood behind the cow shed and this was later turned into a stock yard. Two machinery sheds were built south of this yard and on the west side was a dairy, a bull pen and a wooden barn with a corrugated roof. On the south side was a semidetached property built for farm workers by Mr Sparrow in the 1920's. This was turned into a mixing shed for grinding feed. On the north side of that stood 3 corrugated sheds which were used for the storage of brewers' grain for the cattle feed.

At the bottom of this yard was a lane of established elms, with the Green Lane track running through the bottom of the yard; this track ran from Sutton Road to Eastwood Lodge, and would be used in preference to the low-lying land along Rayleigh Road, as it was less inclined to flood during harsh weather. Land to the south of the brook was Grade One land together with a 14 acre field on Eastwood Rise. This field grew 14 tons of Majestic potatoes to the acre and the farm also grew spring cabbage and wheat, barley, oats and peas, lucerne, kale, mangolds and other cattle feed.

Mr Taylor took over the tenancy in 1949; Bert Redland lived here and worked for Mr Taylor who, in the late 1950's, sold it to the Avery brothers. 12 acres have been compulsorily purchased by Rochford District Council and have been planted with saplings to continue the millennium park westwards; this will be known as New England Wood.

The remaining land is currently farmed by Rankin Farms of Stambridge.

7a. NEW ENGLAND FARM

This farm was not actually in Eastwood but part of Rochford, standing on the north side of the Roach Brook which still marks the boundary between the two parishes. A former 19th century owner was hanged for stealing sheep. The farm covered 116 acres and was later added to Flemings Farm.

8. BLATCHES

Blatches Farm today

This was an Essex County Council holding. It was farmed by Mr Dean until 1942. Then Higgs Crawford farmed it until the 1960's, after which Mr Shiel started a Pick-Your-Own business for soft fruit and so on. There were 110 acres in 1755 but in 1801 this had reduced to 101 acres. Mr Gaines sold the bungalow and the pumping station. A smallholding stood on the north-eastern corner of Blatches Chase, joining up with Blatches Farm. This was occupied by Mr Rumble. Bymr Dean Farm was taken into Hawkwell Parish in 1933 in a boundary change.

Blatches Farm 1977

9. CHERRY ORCHARD

Cherry Orchard Farm was owned by Southend Estates, and farmed by Mr Fowler of Cockethurst Farm. There was a cattle store, and some arable was grown. It also had brick earth kilns adjoining bridleway 10. These 45 acres were excavated for brick earth and then returned for agriculture.

10. WEST BARROW HALL

John Bullock weighing up potatoes at West Barrow Hall - 1960's

West Barrow Hall is now no more than a mound to the north-east of the airport, and is partly owned by a fishing club, but has had a long history. The farm covered 145 acres at its best, in 1899, and its main crops were wheat, barley, oats, sugar beet and peas, sometimes a ley of clover and lucerne. The labour force for pea-picking at West Barrow and at Cherry Orchard Farm came from around the Bellhouse Lane area; the women pickers would be conveyed to and from the farm by lorry.

There was a small amount of meadow land to the farm; sheep and young cattle were grazed there. On one occasion in the 1950's when the cattle were being penned up for tuberculosis testing by the vet, a heifer took fright and jumped the hedge. She ran and kept running, and lived for several weeks in the wooded area of Eastwood. Several people reported seeing her but she was very elusive and avoided being taken back. Then to everyone's great surprise, she eventually turned up back in the meadow. Presumably she came back the same way she had escaped – over the hedge!

The farm had reduced to 114 acres by 1956, when it was sold to Southend Borough Council at auction for £20,000. There was a good weatherboarded barn at West Barrow, with a fine timbered roof, and an unusual, thatched two-horse stable; both were burned down by vandals in the early 1960's

West Barrow Hall

Past owners of west Barrow Hall Farm are known to have taken part in 'The Whispering Court' in Rochford, and it seems to have also been known as Barton Manor and Bregg Hall at various times in the past.

It has been owned by the Bentall family, and farmed by Cecil Hurst. James Tabor of Tabor Farms owned it in 1849, and it seems to have been owned by the Tabor family up to the 1930's.

11. WILDERNESS FARM

This was a mixed farm of 117 acres, split into three units, next to West Barrow Hall Farm and north-east of the current site of the airport. It is believed to be the site of the first planes which flew from the local area. Access was from the Church Lane which ran to the north of St Laurence and All Saints church. Cecil Hurst grazed his sheep here and at West Barrow as well as on the airport, to keep the grass short for the small planes in the early days. He also took hay from there, as did H H Smith in 1954. Sheep were still grazing there up to 1956, the same year that West Barrow Farm went under the hammer.

12. THREE ASHES FARM

This farm stood in Sutton Road, which is now part of Rochford, although it was originally in the parish of Eastwood. It was an inn long before 'The Anne Boleyn' was built, and the licence to sell ale was transferred to the 'Anne Boleyn' when it opened. The farmer in 1927 was Edward Pratt, and in 1933 was F C Horner.

The farm was 52 acres, and stood on the south side of Sutton Road, about 100 yards from where 'The Anne Boleyn' stands now, but was transferred to the north side of the road when the housing estate was erected.

In the 1930's, it was owned by the Marshall family, who also owned Essex and Kent Farmer' wholesale greengrocers, but it was actually farmed by Mr Rumble.

The other main farm wholesaler in the 1930's was W H West and Sons.

Two views of Three Ashes Farm

12A. PURDEYS FARM

Purdey's Farm covered 42 acres and during the 1914-1918 War it was farmed by Bill Jackaman. Towards the end of the war, ex-servicemen were retrained in farming methods for all kinds of agricultural activities, and Bill was foremost locally in this branch of training. After their training, these men were then able to take advantage of a scheme to rent Essex County Council 30-acre smallholdings.

Sid Jackaman succeeded Bill, farming into the 1920's and then part of the farm became a brickfield, known as 'Featherby's', and this also had a loading wharf that is still in use today on the River Roche. As digging progressed, and the sites filled with water, the site became known as 'Jackaman's Ponds'.

A Painting of Purdey's Farm'

On the west side of the farm stood the farmhouse and buildings. Opposite Mill Beach, there had been experimental building of concrete boats, the precursor of the Mulberry Harbour used in World War ll. H. H. Smith had two of the first solid-tyred lorries in Southend to transport bricks from Featherby's.

Next the site was bought by Mr Cater, who kept a very good garden, and who put in the little model railway line which was later moved to Charles Tabor at Sutton Hall. Purdey's was then bought by Claude Mead of Benton Sand and Ballast in 1955 for £3000. After they had worked out the sand and ballast, Benton's moved on to Barling, and the site became the Council tip. Benton, who lived in High Road, Hockley, sold out to Rose Construction, who created Purdey's Industrial Estate. Rose also owned the Glebe in Eastwoodbury Lane, and later built the industrial estate which stands behind the St Laurence Church Hall.

13. HARP HOUSE FARM

The 20 acres of Harps Farm lay on the apex of Manners way and Rochford Road. In 1927, a Mr Charles Phillips is listed in Kelly's Directory as living there. Ray and Eileen Brown lived in the house and George Belcham, Beryl Smith's father, rented the farmland for grazing his horse. The site was sold to Southend Borough Council, so that prefabs (prefabricated houses) could be erected as well as other Council housing.

14. WHITES FARM

This farm was 135 acres. It lay opposite Feeches Road, where the Rochford Road is today, and it was farmed by Bentall's. In the 1930's it became Bentall's housing estate, based on Manners Way. Mr Manners was the main builder for the estate. Smith and Draper built houses, shops and flats either side of The Bell Hotel. Semi-detached house were sold for £500 and a semi-detached bungalow went for £350. The block of flats and shops that stand on the corner of Oaken Grange Drive and Manners Way were split in half in a German bombing raid during World War Two, but there were no casualties and the greater part of the building was left standing. It is believed that the German pilot mistook the building for part of the aerodrome buildings.

15. FEECHES FARM

Feeches Road still exists to remind us of the name of the farm of 143 acres that once stood here. It was west of Whites Farm and Rochford Road and was on both sides of the Arterial Road, up to Eastwoodbury Lane. The land around Feeches road was sold to individual builders once the farm itself was bought by Essex County Council. Prince Avenue Primary School was built on the south side, as well as a block of police houses further west along the A127. The Eastwoodbury Lane end was made into Essex County Council smallholdings along most of its length. The remainder was used as Council housing along the Rochford Road.

16. WHITE HOUSE FARM

The farmhouse and farm buildings stood on the west side of Blatches Chase and there were 110 acres in all. Either side of Blatches Chase were cherry orchards belonging to White House Farm. Land on the east side was bought by Essex County Council for Big West Farm, and it was farmed by Alderman Court. The west side adjoined Dandie's Farm, south of White House Lane. The house still stands on the south side of Whitehouse Road, a short distance from Rochford Corner.

17. BIG WEST FARM

Big West Farm stood on the east side of Blatches Chase. In 1927 Alfred Edward Rumble lived here, possibly as a tenant farmer. The 90-acre Big West Farm was formerly three 30-acre smallholdings owned by Essex County Council, each later farmed by Sid Jackaman and his sons, Ron and Roy until the 1960's. They also owned 30 acres of adjoining land, all Grade One farming land, as in much of Eastwood, and there were stock as well as arable fields here. Big West Farm was demolished in the early 1970's although the smallholding bungalow still stands today. The playing area off Western Approaches was once part of Big West Farm, and was constructed after the land was sold to Southend Council for £3,000,000, thereafter carrying heavy interest charges until the building trade began to expand again after a slump.

Roy Jackaman driving Michael Bull, son of Bob Bull - Smallholder

18. DANDIES FARM

At 194 acres, Dandies' was one of the largest farms in the area. Mr Fowler farmed here, both stock and arable. Potatoes were grown here and they also had a milk and dairy herd. The house stood on the north side of the farmland.

When Mr Fowler died in the 1948, the land south of Green Lane was purchased by Lesley Fellowes for development. The family still own land to the north of the farm itself. Fellowes built a new farm to replace Dandies Farmhouse, which was an Essex timbered farmhouse building which burnt down. There was also a new milking shed and farm buildings and he purchased a Friesian registered herd of over 30 cows which was known as 'The Nobles Green Herd'. This was sold on 19th November, 1969, when the cowman retired.

Dandies Farm blaze

Bill of sale

One man did the milking and ran the farm for 6 or 7 years. Then there was a farm sale. In official words, 'they were averaging 12827 lbs, 3.74% butterfat in 384 days', quite an outstanding feature of the herd at the time of that last sale. Henry Smith bought the bull calves for beef stock. He saw the herd sold on the 19th, November, 1969, by auction. This is believed to be the last milking herd in Eastwood. Offin, Rumsey and Hilliard were the auctioneers based at 22, South Street, Rochford. The Southend Borough boundary was moved north at the house and cow sheds, which fell into disrepair, and large detached properties have been built on the site. Farmland to the north is still retained by the family.

19. HILL FARM

Hill Farm covered 117 acres on the north side of Nobles Green. Percy Wallace and Rupert Hann worked on the farm. Rupert was an ex-jockey. Mrs Richins had a dairy and pig farm. She also rented 15 acres from Sparrow as part of Flemings Farm. This is now a 5-berth caravan site looking over the Roche Valley. Some land was either side of Flemings Lane. (See photograph of house and car). The remainder of the land ran down to Rayleigh Road behind some houses. This land was also bought by Lesley Fellowes, the property developer. The Essex weatherboarded house was pulled down, and new houses and bungalows were built to replace it.

Hill Farm

20. BARKERS FARM

Barkers Farm was opposite the original Victorian Eastwood School building and adjoined Cockethurst Farm. It was owned by Mr Fowler of Cockethurst Farm and the farmhouse was an Essex weatherboard construction. The original Eastwood Primary School building was demolished once the new school was built on the site of Barker's Farm to the east. The new senior school was able to expand into the space.

21. COLEMAN'S FARM

This farm was on the ridge between Prittle Brook and the Arterial Road and covered 275 acres. Hobleythick Lane is to the east, the arterial road to the north and Prittlewell Chase to the south. Southend General Hospital and St Peter's church in Eastbourne Grove were both built on the site of Coleman's Farm. The name continues on in Coleman's Avenue. The housing estate and other developments were begun from the 1920's.

Barkers Farm

22. HIGHLANDS FARM

This farm was in Leigh but was one that was owned by the Bentall Family. A Pendril Bentall owned the land in 940AD, and even the name of Pendril has been passed down into the current generation! Westcliff High School now stands on the site occupied by this farm.

23. BRICKHOUSE FARM

Brick House Farm covered 117 acres. It was an all-grass farm, supporting sheep and was roughly where the Mountdale Gardens area is now. It was farmed from the 1880's by Hugh Bentall. Where the fire station is today marked the southern boundary, and the Children's Centre, built in 2009, also stands on the site of Brickhouse Farm. Playing fields to the north would have joined Picketts Farm to the west. The land also went down to the arterial road. In 1936 Henry Smith's uncle lived at the bottom of Cockethurst Avenue, (now Bridgwater Drive) and Henry remembers seeing Hugh Bentall walking with his black Labrador in order to inspect his sheep. It is believed that the Pest House stood on the bottom of his land, east of Kent Elms Corner. St Cedd's church was also built on this land.

24. PICKETTS FARM

A 62-acre farm, based where Coombes Corner is today, and running southwards towards Leigh, along hat is now Elmsleigh Drive. H Welton, a carman, contractor, farmer and dairyman, lived here in 1929. He is recorded as being paid 24/- (24 shillings = £1.20) per day for ploughing. His activities as a carman meant that he could use his horse and cart to move people and their belongings from place to place.

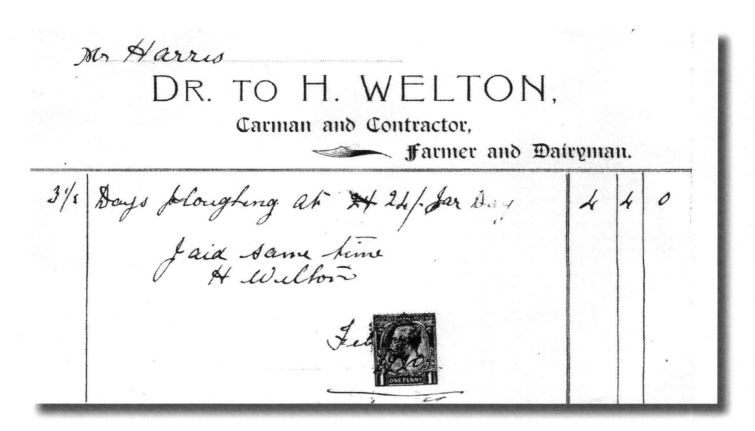

Bill for ploughing.

25. LITTLE PICKETTS FARM

At only 10 acres, this must have been one of the smallest farms in the parish. Lady Sparrow once lived in the house and owned the yard and the 10 acres. It is believed that this was once part of Picketts Farm, but it could have been a convenient place for Lady Sparrow's groom to keep her pony and trap as it was not far from Leigh itself, where she was Lady of the Manor.

26. WOOD FARM

A little bigger then Little Pickett's at 17 acres in 1790 and still 17 acres in 1932, this farm went from Coombes Corner towards Bellhouse Lane, which is now known as Bellhouse Road. In 1936, the Anderson family lived in Kathleen Villa, part of the farm which became the Crescent Timber Yard.

27. BELLHOUSE FARM

Bellhouse Farm covered 117 acres in 1790. A baronet lived there in 1740, when the farm was surrounded by woodland. There were planks across the Eastwood Brook to allow access. In the early 20th Century, the farm was turned over to brick making; it became Cornish's brickfield, specialising in red brick and ornamental bricks. The former office still stands in Rayleigh Road, opposite Dandie's Drive; it looks like a very small bungalow. The kilns stood on the east side of the house before it became the Bellhouse Pub. All the farmland and brickfield to the south has been used for housing.

Bellhouse Farm

The Bellhouse today

28. BELFAIRS FARM

Belfairs Farm was bought by Southend Borough Council for golf club and course in 1922. The farmhouse is still lived in today. The farm buildings and yard are used for storage of Council equipment for the maintenance of the golf course. The area also includes Belfairs riding school, which has a house, coach house and stables, with a trotting track right round the wood, and a separate cycle track. There is an indoor disabled riding school that was opened by Princess Anne. Belfairs Lodge, previously known as Furzefield House, is now the club house and restaurant. There is an old central track from the white gate in Poors Lane to the farm with a road taking you out at Eastwood Road North. There is also a nature reserve to the west.

29. PRIORY FARM

Priory Farm consisted of 134 acres, which included 26 acres of arable and 42 acres of woodland containing 6 cottages and the Priory, the lawns, the greenhouse and a small park. The farm lay either side of Priory Crescent. A farming diary kept by Mr Hurst states that the Prittlewell Priory and the surrounding 30 acres of parkland were given to Southend in perpetuity in 1913 by Mr R. A. Jones, who owned the largest jewellers shop in Southend High Street as well as the Priory Farm Estate. The front of his shop was destroyed by bomb damage in World War Two. Priory Park was officially opened in 1920 by the Duke of York, later King George VI.

29A. EARLS HALL MANOR FARM

Earl's Hall Manor Farm

The 117 acres of Earls Hall Manor were owned by Percy Bentall in the 20th Century, but in 1600, the manor is recorded as being owned by the Earl of Oxford, which could be where it got its name. The coat of arms of the Earl of Oxford was mounted on the chimney stack of the building in the picture. The Earl's Hall Estate is named after the manor farm which originally stood here. The western side of the manor is where Southend Boys' High School and playing fields stand today, adjoining Hobleythick Lane and Prittlewell Chase. The original Priory School was built on this land; this later became the Baptist Church. The farm was linked with Priory Farm, and the manor itself stood on the corner of Victoria Avenue and the lane opposite the current main entrance to Priory Park, now known as Burr Hill Chase.

Earl's Hall Farmhouse

Earl's Hall Manor - South view

Tudor Rochford Hall

30. ROCHFORD HALL

Rochford Hall was far and away the largest farm within the parish of Eastwood. It was estimated at 408 acres in 1867(See Alwin/Cecil Hurst) owned by Tabor's and farmed by Hugh and Arthur Bentall as tenant farmers until 1930. As can be seen from the many mentions of his name in the above writing, Bentall was a major farmer in the area. His family goes back to Pendril Bentall, mentioned in AD 940 as the administrator for the Rochford Hundred Parishes, which was updated in 1100 AD. He was also administrator for Eastwood and Foulness. A descendant of the family, also named Pendril Bentall, still carries on the family tradition of farming today at Little Wakering Wick. Arthur Bentall was the NFU (National Farmers' Union) assessor for a period; Cecil Hurst took over from him in the 1950's or 1960's.

In 1867, James Tabor, the great-great-grandfather of Charles Tabor, bought the Rochford Hall Estate at auction:-

Lot 1 - Large Farm with dilapidated mansion near the church	£25,000
Lot 2 – Brick Kiln Farm, 121 acres, adjoining	
Lot 3 – 68 acres	£9000
Lot 4 – barn yard and buildings – 27 acres	£1300
Lot 8 – opposite Rochford Hall, 5 acres	£600
Lot 9 - opposite Rochford Hall, 237 acres	£1300
Lot 33 – Sutton Temple Farm, 353 acres	£1800
Lot 35 – close to lot 33, 1 acre	£150

At the start of the war, in 1939, F J Hurst & Sons farmed the land at Rochford Hall and at Hylands farm in Hullbridge. Land to the east of the railway line, near to the Anne Boleyn public house was part of Rochford Hall Estate, and was farmed by the Hurst Family into the 1950's. It was given up due problems of theft and security.

Most of the picking was undertaken by women, and the top workers could load up to 46 cwt (hundredweight) of potatoes on a working day. Potato pickers were oftenm paid weekly, and pea pickers were paid by the day.

With the need to intensify food production, other land was taken on in Dollyman's and Beke Hall Farms, Rayleigh as well as Home Farm in Hockley. Labour was increased with the help of Land Girls billeted at 'Winter's', and with German, Italian and Polish prisoners-of-war. A bomb fell in Rochford Hall farmyard early in the war, and others fell on the Aerodrome's Wilderness field, in front of horses with a cart-load of straw. Some of the land belonging to Rochford Hall was lost to the airport and some to the railway during the 20th Century.

In 1944, the first ploughing match was held by the instigation of Cecil Hurst and W. Squire on behalf of the Wartime Agricultural Committee, and these were later taken over by the Rochford Hundred Agricultural Society.

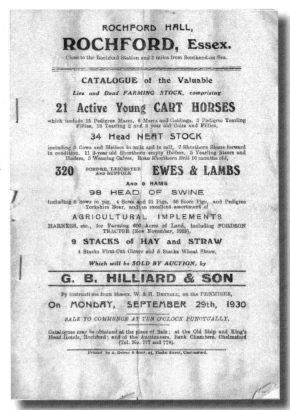

Rochford Hall bil of sale - 1930

Cecil Hurst and his family were the last family to live and work at the Hall, from 1930 until his retirement in 1972. The early and untimely death of Cecil's son, Oswald, brought an end to active farming. The family lived in part of the old manor house, which goes back to the 12th Century and stood in Eastwood Parish.

Rochford Hall cattle yard

Today, Rochford Hall is farmed by Charles Tabor, but is part of the golf club, which is itself over a hundred years old. Rochford Hall has been the home of the famous, including Lord Rich, who enlarged the building, added the tower to the church and endowed the ancient almshouses; then the Boleyn family, whose daughter Anne married Henry VIII and was mother of the first great Queen Elizabeth and whose other daughter Mary inherited the Hall, which, part destroyed by fire, housed airmen during the war and is now the Rochford Hundred Golf Club.

*Rochford Hall during Cecil Hurst's tenure,
now Rochford Golf Club.*

Threshing at Rochford Hall -1960's

Cecil Hurst at Rochford Hall Farm

Much of the information in this chapter has been gleaned from the 1840 tithe map, and supplemented with information from Henry Smith and Sid Broomfield. Thanks must also go to Alywin Hurst for the information supplied on Rochford Hall.

CHAPTER FIVE
EASTWOOD'S SMALLHOLDINGS

As mentioned in the opening chapter, there were a number of smallholdings in Eastwood, originally 29 altogether. They were created by Essex County Council for veterans of the Great War 1914-1918 and each consisted of 30 acres. The land was purchased from three Eastwood farms; Eastwoodbury, Cockethurst and Feeches. All of them could be seen from the Southend Road (now known as the Arterial Road or the A127) and from Eastwoodbury Lane.

Before he could be granted a smallholding, the applicant was obliged to receive farm training; some received this from Bill Jackaman at Purdey's Farm, whilst others were trained at Chelmsford. These Eastwoodbury Lane veterans were still farming the smallholdings in 1956.

1. Clark, H
2. Hancock, William
3. Franklin, Harold C
4. Franklin, Stanley
5. Whitwell, Kenneth J
6. Leigh, William
7. Franklyn, Henry A
8. Parsons, Chas. E; shopkeeper
9. Robinson, Leonard; poultry farmer
10. Gladwin, Hector
11. Peacock, R T
12. Bumble, J
13. Shorter, G
14. Rivermist Nurseries
15. Rand, Edward G; market gardener
16. Watts, Cornelius; market gardener
17. Knight, Albert
18. Lay, Alfred
19. Dennis, Mrs. G; market gardener
20. Hutley, Alfred C

There were other smallholdings shown in the electoral roll of 1926 in Eastwoodbury Lane, but it is believed that it was mistakenly registered as Rochford Road. At the time Rochford Road was all farmland, and Eastwoodbury Lane had been in existence for hundreds of years. The following smallholdings, though, have remarkably high numberings for a lane with so few dwellings!

246, Eastwoodbury Lane – Driscoll, H
403, Eastwoodbury Lane – Holcombe, G
408, Eastwoodbury Lane – Howard, W

Demolition of smallholdings for extension of runway

There were other 30-acre smallholdings on the Southend Road itself, south of Eastwoodbury Lane. Some of the dwellings are still there today, and the land is used for various purposes, such as turf supplies and gardening requirements. From the Devonshire Estate, now the Brendon Way area, working eastwards, these were allocations which if not fully taken up, were offered to other smallholders for farming use.

Glenwood - Lloyd, John; fruit grower.
Abbeville – McClean Jas (6 acres). In 1934, Joseph Spray was a fruit grower here.
Brannam – McClean A J (6 acres); fruit grower.
Melrose Nurseries – Bagnald F W (6 acres; fruit grower.
Gaza – Dunn, H (20 acres); market gardener and farmer.
Troitsa – Davis E W (8acres); market gardener
Mr A Fox (6 acres)
Orchard Cottage – Davis, Herbert (6 acres). A previous tenant was Edmund Stone.
Thanet Grange – Davis, E J (8 acres).
Miss E Lance also lived here, and a previous tenant was Bob Bull.

Eastermont – Kempster J E. This was a detached house, unlike most of the smallholdings. This smallholding eventually swelled to 50 acres of agricultural land, becoming a farm. Before 1957 Hicks Crawford was the second tenant of this farm; he moved to Blatches Farm, which was an Essex County Council holding, after Mr Dean's retirement, and he farmed there until the 1960's.

On the Southend Road, but further west, Sidney and Alf Stokes each had nurseries providing produce for Covent Garden. Sidney began at Noraville on the Rayleigh Road, and later moved to land on the Southend Road east of Bellhouse Lane. Alf's land was on the Grosvenor Estate, west of Progress Road, which was adjacent to Lower Edwards Hall Farm.

The 1928 Census mentions other examples of the agriculture for which Eastwood was so well-known:-

Entry 74-75; Nobles Green Nurseries; Walter and Lily Burridge
Entry 106; Bell House Nurseries; William Bridge
Entry 177; Priory Farm, Prittlewell; Austin Collingwood
Entry 203; Flemmings Farm; William Crabb
Entry 220; 'HUT', Belgrave Road; John Dale

CHAPTER SIX
COCKETHURST FARM AND ITS MOST FAMOUS INHABITANTS

The Vassall Family

Cockethurst Farm in the 1960's

The earliest record we have of Cockethurst Farm is one that states that John Vassall took up residence at Cockseyhurst, Eastwood, in the last year of the reign of Elizabeth I, that is to say, in 1602 or 1603, and structural changes were made which still remain. It is thought that the house was first built in the early 16th century. Above the stout beams of the drawing room rests a canvas ceiling, made of similar material to the sailcloth of the period. There is an oaken staircase to the first floor, but once there was only a rope ladder which could be pulled up at night! There is a fine cellar, which has been flooded more than once, and a spring once flowed there, providing the occupants with fresh water. This was one of a number throughout the area. There was once a small hidden room in Cockethurst, thought to be a hiding place for the priest during times of religious persecution.

The entire house front, gable ends and chimney stacks are still much as they were over 400 years ago. Before this date, John Vassall had lived in Stepney; he was a member of the Virginia Company of London, a skilled navigator and also a merchant.

The family was of French extraction and owned other properties in France. Part of the oak panelling and carved lions' heads that decorate the house interior reflect those found in the French-owned Vassall properties and are thought to have been used as a family emblem since John Vassall 'brought out of Barbarie a lyon's skinne, which from the snoute to the toppe of the taile, contained one and twenty feet in length'!

Another of John Vassall's claims to fame was that, at his own expense, he fitted out and commanded two warships, called the 'Samuel' and the 'Little Toby', against The Spanish Armada in 1588.

The Essex Countryside magazine printed an article by Wilfrid Monk called 'Eastwood – East of the King's Wood'. In this article he writes of the sanitary arrangements at Cockethurst in its early days as mentioned in the "Quarter Sessions Rolls of 1604, in which we read: 'John Vassal, of Eastwood, was presented for that he had built one pryvie house over one brooke that led from his house to Eastwood church, wherebye the inhabitants were greatly annoyed by reason of tainting the brooke and are driven to seke for water els where to there great trobell.'"

John Vassal was married twice and had several sons and daughters by both of his wives; he is reputed to be the common ancestor for all the Vassalls in England. He returned to Stepney from time to time, and in 1625 he died there of the plague. He was buried in Stepney Parish church on the 13th September, 1625.

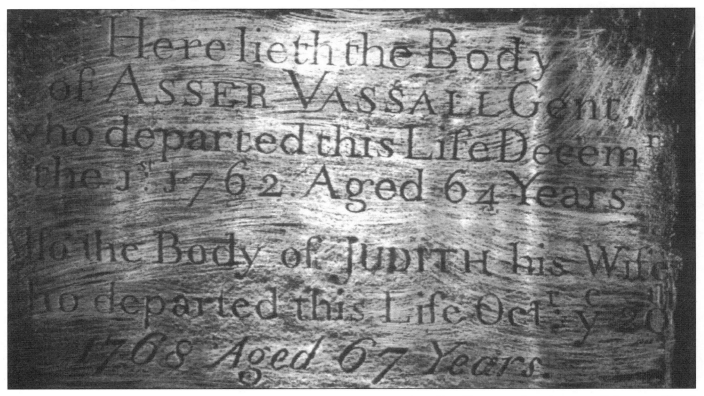

Asser Vassall's memorial can be seen in St Laurence Church

One of John's sons, Asser Vassal, was a friend and neighbour of Samuel Purchas, vicar of Eastwood, and Asser became church warden in 1721. It is presumably during this time that he carved his name into the stone-work of the north doorway!

In 1720, Coxdeheart was rated at £30. The deeds of the farm itself cannot be traced back further than 1752, when Asser Vassall had inherited the property. Asser was one of three known sons. He died in 1808, the last surviving member of the Vassall family locally, and his body was interred in the sanctuary of Eastwood church.

Samuel and William had active interests in the developing colonies of America, and apparently owned 10 % of the city of Massachusetts, New England, by purchase proprietorship, in March, 1628. By September of that same year, Samuel was imprisoned after a conflict with the Custom House, and all his possessions were confiscated. He was in prison until 1636, but three years later, he seems to have had a reversal of fortunes, for in March, 1639, he was elected to represent the City of London in the Short Parliament that sat from April 13th to May 5th. He was later re-elected for the Long Parliament, but it was not until 1656 that recompense was granted in the case.

Some sources attribute a quarter share of 'The Mayflower' to Samuel Vassall, and certainly the Vassall family maintained links with the Puritans and the New England colonies. There was a 'Mayflower' of London, owned by John Vassall and others mentioned in documents in 1594, and The Pilgrims went to America in the 'Mayflower' in 1620. Samuel's nephew became leader of the Puritan movement in Prittlewell and signed the solemn league and covenant against Charles I in September 1643. It is thought that Samuel died in Massachusetts but

Mayflower II - considered to be an exact replica

the exact time and place are not known, although there is a monument to Samuel Vassall in King's Chapel, Boston, Massachusetts.

Asser Vassall's only daughter, Mary, had married William Weld Wren of Southchurch, who was the son of a Prittlewell surgeon, Richard Wren. Mary and her husband moved in to Eastwood Bury, next to the church, which had also been a long-term residence of the Vassall family. In 1830 Mary died, predeceasing her husband by nineteen years, and William moved to Cocket Hurst, where he made further substantial alterations to the house.

The Vassall family continued to contribute to British history through Lady Holland, nee Elizabeth Vassall, a great Regency hostess, and later through John Vassall, a spy in the 1960's.

Another gentleman who was a friend of the Vassall family and resided at Cocksey-Hart was Thomas Hoskins, a lieutenant of the Marines. He is recorded on an oval tablet at Eastwood church and died in 1798, aged 59.

In the early years of the 19th Century, Mr Vassall was recorded as being one of the most important and influential farmers in Eastwood. He farmed three hundred and fifty acres. He found that ploughing in a clover crop gave a greatly increased yield of wheat the next year. We now know that this is due to the extra nitrogen that clover can return to the soil. Cockethurst Farm had thirty acres of meadow and fifty acres of clover. On this, Mr Vassal had one hundred Old Leicester and one hundred Lincoln ewes and one hundred Shearling sheep. His average clip of wool was eight pounds weight, which in 1804 sold for 16d (7pence today) per pound. It was common practice about Rochford to purchase Berkshire hogs at Romford Market and turn them out into the clover fields, but whether this was done at Eastwood is not known.

Cockethurst enters a harvest wagon in to Southend Carnival - 1960's

The Fowler Family

Thomas Fowler

Mrs Orana Fowler, with Mr Cook, of Snakes Lane, a family friend

Cockethurst Farm stayed in the hands of descendants of the Vassall/Wren family until 1913, when it was purchased by the farm bailiff, John Thomas Fowler. It is rumoured that he came to the area from Lincolnshire via Southminster in 1895 with a shovel and a spade across his shoulders.

The Fowler family occupied Cockethurst Farm for most of the 20th Century. During this time the building became a Grade Two Listed building.

John Thomas Fowler was an important man; he was an alderman of Southend, and a great benefactor to the community of Eastwood, as were his four daughters. He had served on Eastwood Parish Council, Essex County Council and the Rochford Rural District Council. He became a Justice of the Peace in 1933, an appointment of which he was very proud, and his last attendance on the bench was the day before he died. He stood as an independent Councillor for Southend-on-sea from 1934, when Eastwood joined the enlarged borough and remained as a Councillor until his death in 1948. He was also a life member of Southend General Hospital and endowed a bed there to commemorate his Golden Wedding Anniversary. He ran his own farm, which was maintained for a while by his widow, Orana and their daughters after his death. Orana was the sister of Cecil Hurst, of Rochford Hall.

All the family attended Eastwood St Laurence church and would arrive in a large chauffeur-driven black car. The ladies would all have matching fur coats and hats, making quite an impact as they walked in to the church. The daughters loved to sing and always tried to out-sing the choir, especially when the song had a descant.

After their mother's death, the daughters, Raine, May, Gladys and Ethel continued to take on the responsibilities of the parish. They donated land for parks, made sure

The FOWLER sisters with their mother.
Photo taken Christmas 1959 at Cockethurst Farm, Eastwood.

Top Left: RAINE FOWLER (twin). Died 16th March 1976 age 80 years.

Top Right: MAY FOWLER (twin). Died 21st May 1975 age 79 years.

Bottom Left: GALDYS FOWLER. Died 7th January 1979 age 77 years.

Bottom Right: ETHEL FOWLER. Died 11th October 1980 age 83 years.

Centre: ORANA FOWLER, Mother. Died 20th February 1961 age 89 years.

(JOHN THOMAS FOWLER. Died 9th March 1948 age 76 years.)

The Fowler Ladies

that the local elderly people were cared for and later gave the colourful west window to St Laurence, showing the history of Cockethurst and all its associations with America and so on. They donated the central heating to the church as well as giving money towards the church upkeep.

None of the sisters ever married. The last two surviving sisters had a house built opposite Cockethurst, called 'Mayflower Lodge' which they wished to retire to, intending that Cockethurst itself should become a home for the elderly, but it was not considered suitable, and so was never accomplished.

The Fowler family tomb is just to the east of the Eastwood St Laurence porch, and the name partially lives on, also, in the naming of a small road by Eastwood Primary School as 'Four Sisters Way'.

The Fowler Ladies liked to dress alike

Councillor Gladys Fowler

Mayflower Lodge - a copy of a bungalow in Chalkwell Avenue

Cockethurst Farm

Despite centuries of having its name spelled in a variety of ways throughout its long history, Cockethurst Farm house has stood the test of time. Although it is in private hands, it remains well-looked after, with manicured lawns and a surround of mature trees including a stand of beautiful horse chestnuts on its south wall. The hedgerow on the road side contains many different varieties of shrub, indicating its great age. The red Tudor brick porch in front of the house seems seldom used, as most of the traffic uses the rear entrance, where the barns have been adapted for the motor car instead of the horse.

Flood at Cockethurst Corner - 1958

In 2002 the Essex Life and Countryside magazine stated that there was still a well beneath the floor of the former kitchen, and that the house still contains some of the original features, including two lion head panels carved into the timber of the dining room fireplace.

One of the downstairs rooms, known as the sailcloth room, features a ceiling of barge sailcloth. It is thought that the original was placed there by Asser Vassall to remind of the seafaring influences in the family, and that some of the timbers used in the porch and some used in St Laurence church may have come from Vassall ships.

A staircase to the upper floor was put in to the house in the 1800's to replace a rope ladder which could be pulled up when all the family had gone up to bed – another remnant of sailing days, no doubt!

During mid-twentieth century renovation, a small room was discovered which one could only access from the attic floor. It was thought to be a priests' hole, or a hiding-place for the family if under threat from cut-throats and ruffians!

Another old feature of the house is the row of servants' bells hanging in the family room (once the kitchen), but obviously a little later than some of the older features of the house. Although the furnishings may have changed considerably in the intervening centuries, there is little doubt that if the Vassals were to return today, they would be delighted to see that very little has changed in their old home after 400 years.

CHAPTER SEVEN
EASTWOOD SCHOOLS

SIR - I wish to draw attention to the urgent need of an elementary school here for hundreds of children, who have to go four miles to and fro to attend a school at Rayleigh, or one on the Leigh-on-sea border-line, the schools being nearly four miles apart, parents having to pay 'bus fares, and the children getting no midday meal. A school could be erected here on the Limehouse Hill, Grosvenor, or Eastwood Lodge Estate for 30/- per head, while £10,000 is to be spent in enlarging the Rayleigh School, at a cost of £50 per scholar's seat. We have nine chapels and halls, twenty crossroads, and five penny 'bus fares between the two schools, and on our rate demands we are charged for elementary, secondary, and high-class education, while there is none in this benighted parish, which adjoins the well-to-do borough of Southend-on-sea.

H.M.WHITE

SIR - Last September, I received a summons to attend the Police Court at Southend for non-payment of half a year's rates in Eastwood Parish. I attended the Court as I wished to draw attention to the absence of a school here for the hundreds of children who have to walk four miles to and fro daily, and go without a midday meal, to attend Rayleigh School, or one on the Leigh-on-sea border line. Thus while we are charged foe elementary, secondary, and high-class education, we have none.

For protesting against this neglect of the Board of Education, I have had to pay 12/- for summons, warrant and committal order, although no execution or warrant had been served upon me, and the six months rates were paid three days before the expiration of the period for which they were made.

H. M. WHITE
Eastwood Lodge Estate, Essex

Mr White had every reason to be irate. The population of Eastwood was increasing fast in the late 19th century due to better farming methods and increased labour bringing a small measure of prosperity to the neighbourhood, and more and more services were required. The farm labourers with their young families were obliged to place their children in school by law, regardless of how far they were obliged to travel in order to do so. It has to be said that we cannot draw judgements based on today's lifestyle, as it was not uncommon then for people to walk several miles to work, and children would be expected to be able to do the same from a very early age, being treated at the time like small adults, waiting to be the same size as their elders.

However, it is beyond dispute, that Eastwood village in the 1870's had more than 40 children in need of an elementary education, in addition to which there was an itinerant population of gypsy children who were not exempt from the law.

The first elementary school finally opened on April 7th, 1879. Eighteen children arrived for school that day, and eight new pupils arrived on the following day. Four weeks later, the school could boast 48 children, and work began on improving their education.

It must have seemed strange to people who had not themselves been schooled to have to send their children off to be trained by others. The former way was for each child to be gradually inducted into the trade or occupation of his father, and very often his grandfather, and so on. But people must have been becoming

Eastwood School stood opposite Barker's Farm

more aware of the changing times under Victoria's rule. The revolutions in industry were forcing more and more people away from their own birthplace, in order to find work. The small cottage industries of spinning and weaving, for instance, had been swept away by factory machines, and those who had formerly eked out an existence from small trades, supplementing their income by keeping a market garden and perhaps a cow, found themselves priced out their homes and having to adopt a new way of life. The population of the whole country had begun to rearrange itself into different formations, and no doubt, Eastwood's growth had a lot to do with these changing times.

Eastwood School corridor - 1950's

However, although the law said that children should attend school, there was still a long way to go in altering the attitudes of the populace! If parents employed on the land were involved in some sort of farm work, it was expected that the children would also be available to lend a hand. For instance, the school log book for September, 1883 records that the headmaster tried to open the school on the 17th but only 9 children came. The following day there were still only 11 children, as all hands were required for the harvest. The roll at this time was around 60 children.

Eastwood was a busy agricultural area, with farms and smallholdings, and orchards full of fruit. The gathering of the harvest was obviously an extremely important part of the lives of the rural community. Not only did the harvest provide local revenue, but individuals were obliged to pot and preserve their ripe produce in preparation for the winter. In the days before each household had its freezer and fridge, these chores would not wait. When the hay was ready, haymaking took place! The children were able, from a very early age, to perform many useful services; they could collect apples, pick soft fruit, help their mothers with the preparation of preserves, push the barrows of produce to the Rochford Market and so on.

Thus the records show that whenever a harvest or crop was ready, the attendance figures, averaged weekly by the headmaster, would drop. By 1883, he was able to say that in early October, the children were absent because of potato lifting. This pattern continued for many years, in spite of all the authorities could do!

The other problem with getting children to school in those early years was the weather. In 1881, the school was closed for a week in mid-January. The roads would not have been so numerous at that time and very few were "made up" with tarmac, so access to the school with its wide catchment area was a real problem. The Rayleigh Road itself was a good road, but most of its contributory roads were still fairly sparsely populated, and the surfaces were deeply rutted in poor weather, and hard to traverse, especially if you add the problem of inadequate footwear as was common amongst the poorer families of the time. No snow-ploughs in the 19th Century!

Eastwood School gardening club 1924

Even the summer was not without its weather problems, as was reported in 1880. The school inspection had taken place on July 29th, and the report was not particularly good. "The order is good", writes the inspector, but "the children were evidently deplorably ignorant"! One would hope that no inspector would be allowed to write that these days, in case of being sued, but then one was apparently allowed to call a spade a spade! The following day, there was a very heavy rain, and only one boy came, so that the school failed to open. There were 32 who registered in the afternoon. Perhaps it was the weather, or maybe it was post-inspection stress!

Later that year, in the autumn, several children failed to turn up at school, due to The Leigh Regatta. Presumably this festival has not always taken place at the weekend, as it does today!

This rather lackadaisical attitude obviously continued for some years. Not only did it seem unimportant to some parents to inform the authorities that their children would be absent, but if their child were to be offered a job whilst under the statutory school leaving age, they would encourage him to take it, regardless of the consequences.

It was only a matter of time before the authorities decided to challenge parental decisions and make an example of some of these recalcitrant families! On the 2nd March, 1900, Mr A. Todd was prosecuted for the non-attendance of his son, 13 years old, who had been at work for about a year without having passed the 4th Standard of Exemption.

> *'The magistrates refused to convict without giving a reason for their decision. After this decision it will be impossible to enforce the attendance of children over 13 who are not legally qualified to leave school'*

As if to make a point, the boy, Archer returned for two days only during the week of the 27th April.

By the first term of 1903, numbers had increased so much that the school managers were beginning to express the opinion that 'the provision of additional accommodation in the neighbourhood of the old workhouse would probably relieve the pressure at the present school.'

Conditions were becoming harder for many, and it is noted that the caretaker, whose name was Mrs Keyes, had resigned. Her wage was 2/- (two shillings) per week in the summer and 3/- per week in the winter. If we try to compare the wage with its modern equivalent of 10p/15p, it sounds ridiculously small. The following year, a new teacher was employed at £50 per annum, and we see that the headmaster was earning £140 per annum, so maybe Mrs Keyes had found better-paid work elsewhere. The differential was enormous. I find it strange that in 1904, a female should be employed as a caretaker for a school, but to date we have found no written explanation for this. She could perhaps have been the widow of the caretaker, fulfilling his work until a replacement could be found.

In 1905, the Infant department of the school was accommodated at the Parish Room. The charge was at first 20/-, but this was increased dramatically by 50% to 30/- when it was discovered that there was a lot of redecorating required at the end of the school year. It was also said that it was very inconvenient for the rest of the community in that they were unable to use the Parish Room for anything else, while it was occupied by the Infants and their teacher.

It was a requirement of all schools in those early days that great attention would be paid to the religious, spiritual and moral development of children. Most children were sent to Sunday school and many attended the Sunday Services with their parents. It was understandable, therefore, that the school log-book refers to the weekly visit of the Reverend Spencer. He would be responsible for conducting an assembly and would visit the classes, often checking on whether individual children had learned their catechism. This would often take the form of a portion from scripture, learned by heart, and repeated to the vicar on request. The usual punishments for not learning your catechism correctly would be a sharp slash on the hand (for girls) or the backside (for the boys) from the cane kept in each classroom.

Eastwood Memorial Hall. Some lessons were held here during refurbishment

The Rev. Spencer was part of the team of people who were the school governors, responsible for the decision-making involved in the education of the Eastwood boys and girls. The other members included H. Bentall, the local farmer and landowner who was the chairman of the governors. He, with his wife and daughter were all part of the management team of the Eastwood School, up till the time of the last available record in May, 1933.

Most of the lessons took the form of rote learning, and there would have been few books for the children to learn from. It was assumed that the teacher, who would have received a good education herself, would be able to impart as much information as was necessary to the children in her care. The 'primers' that the children did have in Victorian times mainly consisted of lists of words, some nonsensical, that followed a pattern, and it was the duty of the older pupils to take care of the rote reading of these words on the part of the younger pupils.

It is strange to note that there is no record in the log book of the end of WWII.

In 1914, a Mr White (could it possibly be the same one?) had written to the school managers to object to the building of a new classroom and suggested a new school midway between Eastwood and Rayleigh.

By June, 1928, numbers had risen to 289 on roll. The children received gardening and cookery lessons in line with current educational policy.

On Christmas Eve 1944, a V2 rocket fell on Park Avenue, narrowly missing the school and several bungalows, but creating a huge amount of damage. The picture of the railings was taken in 2008!

V2 Rocket damage on the school railings

A class at Eastwood School 1953

CHAPTER EIGHT
ST. LAURENCE PLAYERS.

St Laurence Players began towards the end of 1969, when the vicar, Mr Herbert Woolcott, observing that the Saturday Drama Group for young people was such a success, decided to start a similar group for the parents. He even wrote the first play, resulting in the fact that there was no need to pay royalties or fees to a third party. The first performance was given in February, 1970.

From that first idea the St Laurence players grew and flourished, and has provided entertainment to many, as well as encouraging lots of hidden talents to emerge in the realms of music, painting and acting and providing a new interest for a number of local people.

Mr Woolcott's play, The Last Birthday Party, was well reviewed in the local Press. Everyone who had responded to the call to start a drama group was given a part, the ladies, for the most part playing maids and housekeepers, but that small idea blossomed and three more productions were put on the same year, with Old Time Music Hall for Christmas.

Each year after that saw at least two productions by 'The Players' with a serious play followed by pantomimes and Christmas offerings at the end of the year. The Pantomimes were often old favourites; Cinderella, Aladdin, Rapunzel, Sleeping Beauty to name but four!

New play in an old mould

1970

Spring an
Port

de
Seren
melodies
another but
theme never subm
concertos by Charles
and Corelli.

THE LOCAL vicar wrote the whodunnit that over one hundred people saw performed in Eastwood Church Hall last Friday and Saturday (Picture above).

Rev. H. D. Woolcott's story, "The Last Birthday Party," was rooted in classic thriller tradition with its drawing room setting, investigating C.I.D. man and death-dealing local doctor.

The cast, all members of St. Laurence's Church, styled themselves the St. Laurence Players. It was the first time they had acted together.

Though they were all rather stiff in the opening scenes several of them warmed up to give quite creditable performances.

A word of praise for Ken Done as Grandfather, who coped manfully with a plethora of unlikely dialogue.

Of the four brothers, Colin Banks as Timothy and Basil Sheffield as George made the most impression. The former gave the play's best performance and dealt with his part in a relaxed, natural fashion. Mr. Sheffield seemed somewhat tense and anxious to be "acting" all the time.

John Moore was appropriately lean and masterful as the C.I.D. inspector, but his performance would have been smoother had he made his exits less melodramatically. The doctor, John Bambrook, was rather impressive in his one short appearance and the play would have benefited from his presence in other scenes.

The ladies in the cast didn't get much of a look in, save for Beryl Brown — quite a nice performance as an earnest, slow-witted housekeeper.

The general impression was of an embryo group who should have it in them to produce good productions once the inevitable kinks are ironed out.

Others performing were: Ron Fleming, Henry Smith, Sylvia Sheffield, Pat Fleming, Margaret Woolcott, Jean Banks and Robert Lewis. Patricia Smith produced.

TIM STOUT

New play, old mould.: Sylva Sheffield, Jean Banks, Basil Sheffield, Henry Smith, Margaret Woolcort, Ken Doone, Beryl Brown, John Barnbrook, Colin Banks, Pat Flemming, Ron Flemming, Bob Lewis, John Moore.

In 1977 there was a production of Trial and Error, a deep murder mystery, carried out with aplomb by the cast. In June, the Queen's Jubilee was celebrated with 'Jubilee Revels' with a cast of old and young members. Many of the original players are still doing their bit to entertain the good folk of Eastwood. In 2000, the year began with a Show Stoppers Review, with a well-produced rendition of items from 'Oliver Twist', and in 2006, the team tackled with gusto two Agatha Christie plays, including 'Hickory, Dickory Dock', a Hercule Poirot story. Once again, audiences were extremely appreciative of how well they were done.

The St Laurence Players' have taken part in Southend Carnival and have performed at the Nurses Home in the old Rochford Hospital. A big, shiny, 'glass' coach was built for Cinderella, but sadly it fell from its transport on Warners Bridge and was swept away by the Corporation!

There are many people who have been a part of 'Players since its inception by Rev Woolcott, and some deserve a special mention. Sadie and Stan Smith and Tricia Smith did some great work with the Young Players; accompanists, Mary Baylis, Harry Marsh, David Stanley, Derek Wyeth; Kathy, Mabel, Irene, Marion, Audrey, Joanie, Lewis and Basil; all have played their parts to the best of their abilities,

The Programmes so far.

1970	February	The Last Birthday Party.
	June	Mid-summer interlude, and The Bathroom Door.
	October	Harvest Supper and The Stunt.
	December	Olde Tyme Music Hall and The Dear Departed.
1971	June	Here we come Gathering.
	December	Christmas Show '71.
1972	May	I'll get my man.
	December	Christmas Show '72.
1973	June	Love from a Stranger.
1974	June	Kentucky Revels.
	October	Love's a Luxury.
1975	June	Count your Blessings.
1976	January	Music Hall
	June	Too soon for Daises.
	December	Belle Star's Western Showdown

Jubilee Revels 1977.
Andy Ragget, Irene Sharpley Stan Smith, Michael Sheffield, Nellie Wood Masie Baylis, Mr. Ragget, Sadie Smith, Colin Banks, Joan Boiling, Jimmy Amour, Mabel Free, Will White, Frances Banks, Tricia Smith Sharon Elvidge Jackie Elvidge, Henry Smith, Shelia Elvidge, Jean Banks, Linda White.

1977	April	Trial and Error.
	June	Jubilee Revels.
1978	January	From Carriages to Concorde
	June	With Vacant Possession.
	December	Christmas Show '78.
1979	April	Night must Fall.
	December	Cocktail Capers.

Back row: Henry Smith Andy Ragget, Stan Smith, Will White, Jimmy Armour.
Front Row: Michael Sheffield, Colin Banks.

1980	April	Pickle in Paradise.
	December	Christmas Crackers.
1981	May	Suspect.
	December	Christmas Crackers.
1982	May	Breath of Spring.
	December	Christmas Crackers.

Eastwood Ladies
Shelia Elvidge, Jean Banks, Linda White, Alyson Buries, Bertie Ladd, Beryl Brown Irene Sharpley, Kathy Bover.

1983	April	Anyone for Tennis.
	July	Midsummer Madness.
	December	Babes in the Wood.

TeleTubbies
Colin Banks, Bryan Darby, Alan Ladd, Roland Stanley.

1984	May	Midsummer Mink
	December	Christmas crackers.
1985	May	Moonshine.
	November	Christmas Crackers.
1986	May	A Play??
1987	September	Stranger in the House.

Oliver Twist;
Colin Banks, Bertie Ladd, Peter Chandler, Betty Boote, Bryan Darby, Claire, Frances Banks, Kathy Bover,
Linda White, Alan Ladd, Jean Banks.

1988	May	Patient in 4B.
	December	Mother Goose.
1989	May	A Murder is Announced.
	December	All clean fun.

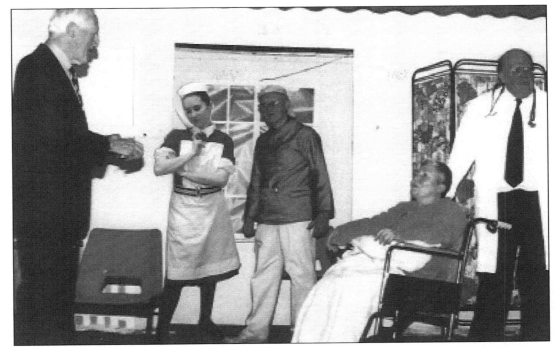

Agatha Christie.
Basil Sheffield, Vikki Murray, Ron Biggins, Jean McKenzie, Roland Stanley

1990	May	Busybody.
	December	Olde Tyme Music Hall
1991	May	Fish out of Water.
	November	Christmas Show. Here we are again.
1992	November	Christmas Show.
1993	May	Green Fingers
	December	Christmas Show.
1994	May	Off The Deep End.
	December	Xmas Show Stardust '94.
1995	May	Peace Party
1996	May	Spring Tonic, Plays and Music.
	December	Cinderella.
1997	December	Aladdin.
1998	May	Musical Selections.
	December	Rapunzel.
1999	December	Sleeping Beauty.
2000	May	Show stopper review.
	September	Celebration Street Party.
2001	January	Puss in Boots.
2002	January	Red Riding Hood.

2003	January	O.K. Corral.
2004	January	Pinocchio.
2005	January	Dick Whittington.
2006	January	Hickory, Dickory, Dock.
	April	2 Agatha Christie Plays
	December	Humpty Dumpty.
2007	April	Plays and Music
	December	Dracula.
2008	January	Burns Nite.
	May	Spring into Summer, 2 Plays and Music.
	August	Proms in the Park.
	December	Bobby Shaftoe
2009	May	4 Plays and music.
	August	Proms, Buddy Holly.
	December	Ali Baba.
2010	May	Spring Show, 2 Plays and music
	July	Proms in the Park, Walt Disney
	December	Old King Cole in Space. Cancelled, weather.
2011	January	Panto as above.
	May	Spring Show, plays and music
	July	Summer Show.
	October	Beetle Drive
2012	January	Snow White and some small people.

CHAPTER NINE
THE AIRPORT

Southend Flying Club actually began using gliders on the site of an old pony racecourse north of Dalys Road in Rochford in 1929, although there is some evidence that it may have begun as early as 1912.

The club persuaded Southend Council to buy the present site, and in March 1935, the club moved in with a membership of about 200. A hangar, restaurant, workshops and a club house were built, and the aerodrome was officially opened on September 18th, 1935, by Sir Philip Sassoon, the Under Secretary of State for Air. Flying was becoming more common, and support from the public was shown at the annual 'Open Day' where a number of aviation- related activities took place.

As early as the summer of 1937 the Royal Air Force sent at least one squadron of fighter aircraft to the aerodrome and in 1938, spectators were treated to a display of the new Spitfire, which had first flown in 1936. It was in 1938 that the aerodrome became fully operational, and at the outbreak of war, it was fully requisitioned and became 'RAF Rochford'. In 1936, the aerodrome had taken more land, and in 1939, adopted all the land up to the Golf Club boundary, the land then being undersown with grass.

German reconnaisance map from WWII

When the war started, 'RAF Rochford' became operational as a satellite station to Hornchurch Aerodrome Some areas of the golf course were ploughed up to grow wheat, and other parts were used to erect tents for airmen and soldiers. A large decontamination unit was built close to Duffers Bank at Rochford Hall. 'Pillboxes' and other defences were erected, including single scaffold poles with wire stretched between to deter enemy aircraft from landing.

At this juncture, all civilian flying ceased. Private aircraft were either pressed into RAF service or stored locally.

'RAF Rochford' was mainly used as a forward base for fighter aircraft operations, and in October, 1940, the name was changed to 'RAF Southend'. It played a key role in the Battle of Britain and in the D-Day landings. Aircraft operating from here were credited with being the first single-seat aircraft to shoot down an enemy aircraft over England, and at least two enemy aircraft crash-landed on the site. Squadrons manned by British, Norwegian, Polish, Belgian and Czech pilots operated a variety of fighter and communications aircraft.

The site was continually adapting during the War years, and many defensive structures were built, including a three-storey gun-tower situated at the junction of Eastwoodbury Lane and Bristol Road.

Southend Airport received its licence to operate once the RAF had left, in December, 1946, with the Council committing itself to developing the airport as an international gateway. In 1948 Customs facilities were established for the new services to Ostend by East Anglian Flying Services Ltd.

Anti-aircraft HQ. Eastwood

During 1949, Aviation Traders Ltd formed to convert ex-military aircraft into cargo planes, and the site was used extensively as a storage facility for war-surplus aircraft. The legendary Freddie Laker was in charge at this time, and appeared to have laid the foundations for his empire among the aircraft being stored or scrapped at Southend airport.

In 1954, in spite of opposition from certain areas of the town most likely to be affected by increasing the number of commercial flights, Southend Council replaced the grass runways with two permanent concrete runways. By the end of the Nineteen-Fifties, 200,000 passengers were using the airport for flights including day trips to France!

In 1962, the first Carvair flew from Southend; this carried cars and passengers. By 1967, the numbers of passengers had peaked at nearly 700,000.

Passenger numbers in the 1970's declined steadily from nearly 472,000 in 1971 to just over 200,000 in 1979. The early 1970's saw Channel Airways go into liquidation, and Aviation Traders moved to Stansted.

The Historic Aircraft Museum opened its doors in 1974, but was not destined to last; freight figures dropped in 1977 to the lowest for 23 years; the last Carvair was retired in 1979 – not a good decade for the airport.

Then in 1981, it was seen that BAF had become the world's largest operator of Viscount aircraft; with package tours to Italy, Malta and Yugoslavia, organised by Cosmos Holidays, Horizon and Burstin Travel, Southend Airport was rated the fourth busiest in the UK by 1988.

Open Day 1968

The lease of the Airport was sold to Regional Airports Ltd in 1994, and thus another decline set in. It was sold on to the Eddie Stobart transport group in 2008, and in the four years following the purchase a new station has been built by the airport, a 300-bed hotel is in process, and an enlarged passenger terminal has been built to cater for 2 million passengers a year. At this time, the owners have applied for, and gained, an extension to the runway, and once again, large passenger planes are flying in and out of the airport, with plans from the owners to expand to 6 million passengers per year if there is no opposition.

The 1970's aircraft museum

CHAPTER TEN
SOME LAST THOUGHTS

In 1953, the Milton Hall Brick company, working at Cherry Orchard Lane uncovered graves dating back to AD 120-140. They found several artefacts there, including Samian ware platters and cups, an iron lamp holder, beakers, glass flagons, nails and animal bones, indicative of a settlement nearby. Betwenn 1953 and 1956, three further cremation burial groups were found, together with evidence of Iron age occupation.

The Domesday Book tells us that in 1086 there were sufficient woods in Eastwood to sustain 50 swine, which by today's reckoning amounts to 250 acres of woodland. In the 13th Century, St Paul's Cathedral undertook a large-scale survey of the property owned by the church, and recorded that a wood was given to the church by Sr. James de Eastwood in1251.

Westminster Abbey was next to record details of the woods that they owned, and they wrote details of who was managing them and what work was being carried out. Geoffrey Dersham and Thomas Ocle, a 14th Century vicar of St Laurence were recorded as 'cutting down and selling a suitable amount of underwood in the Kings parks and woods of Haddele, Rayleigh and Thunderle' and to deliver any residue to the Clerk of Works for the repairing of Hadleigh Castle, which was being extended in the 1360's.

In 1322, William de Rothwell, the current Parson of St Laurence, successfully claimed tithe of the foals coming out of Rayleigh Park.

In 1361, John Holbecke received the King's permission to pasture 14 cows in Rayleigh Park, an increase on the the previous allowance of 8 cows and 12 pigs, and then later in 1401, the men of Eastwood were allowed pasture for 20 cattle and pannage for 20 pigs.

WHAT'S IN A NAME?

Harp House roundabout at the junction of Manners Way and Warners Bridge
was named for John Le Harpe, of Harp House in Eastwood, the owner in 1374.

Eastwoodbury Lane - In the 17th Century Bradford Bury owned Eastwood-lodge and Edwards-hall, and lived at Eastwood-bury. His son Henry is recorded in addition as owner of White-house.

William Meakens and his son James, of Little Wakering are also recorded as owners of White-house, hence Whitehouse Road.

Wren Avenue, named for William Weld Wren who Inherited Cockethurst by marriage to Mary Vassall.

Macmurdo Road named for Gilbert Macmordy of Rochford, owner of West Barrow Hall.

Symons Avenue, named for Symon Channells.

A small farm on Nobles Green, sold in 1757 to Saffory , for whom Saffory Close was named.

Nobles Green, named for John Nobull, 1482.

Picketts Avenue, named for Henry Pycot, 1304.

Blatches Chase for Richard Blatche, (no date).

Flemings; Thomas Fflemynge ,1578.

These are definitely some names to conjure with, but probably no more outstanding than any other landowners from previous centuries. It is good to know that some of the history of Eastwood has continued by preserving these ancient names. The latest historical name to join this long line is the name of the Fowler Sisters, preserved now in the naming of Four Sisters Way, leading to the estate of houses built where Barkers Farm once was, and owned by John Thomas Fowler, of Cockethurst Farm, the father of four daughters, Raine, May, Gladys and Ethel. (See Chapter Six)

The ancient map on the wall of the North aisle of the church shows the original boundaries of the parish of Eastwood in 1840, and shows how vast the parish once was. The Horse and Groom pub is marked and is reputed to be a place where tenants of landlords outside of Eastwood received their rents. Tithes for Eastwood were paid to the Bailiff of the Manor at Rochford Hall. The Eastwood parish went up to the boundary with Sutton parish, and the boundary between Eastwood and Rochford was defined by the River Roach.

Gone from the bend in the road to the east of the church is the old-fashioned blue police box, which had a telephone which the general public could use to report incidents direct to the police station in the days before everyone possessed a phone at home.

Gone are the stables, pig sties, barns and sheds which stood, amongst other farm buildings by Eastwoodbury Cottages, which used to house farm workers' families. They had stood there for hundreds of years. The cottages themselves are now earmarked for demolition to accommodate the proposed extension to the runway of the airport.

Gone too is Carthouse Cottage, a wooden two level building which looked like a cottage on top of a garage. This was a very common type of house, with living accommodation above and workshop below. Carts and traps used by the Stallibrass Family, owners of the Manor House which stood at the end of the sweeping drive that led to Eastwood Bury, or Bury Priory, were repaired and sometimes housed here up to World War Two. During the war, it was used by the air force but after the war it was used to house homeless families. It was demolished to make way for the extension to the airport runway.

Also gone now is the little lane behind the church lane leading to a group of black boarded cottages (Church Cottages) where Rose Nunn, the Church Caretaker, lived. She was by all accounts a formidable lady who was a source of all knowledge regarding Eastwood. Grace Panton's father, John Porter, had known her since they were both young and was allowed to call her Rosie, but such familiarity was not encouraged or allowed to everyone.

Gone are the businesses that flourished in the smallholdings along Eastwood bury Lane. Some smallholders specialized in soft fruits such as strawberries, raspberries, gooseberries etc. Others sold eggs and poultry. There were orchards, vegetables, flowers, pig farmers, poultry, plants, and, just before Avro Road, No.8. Smallholdings had a small shop which was run by Mrs. Parson and then Mr. & Mrs. Clarke.

The wartime concrete fortifications are gone, but once again, there are road names which remind us of early aviation names; Wells, Vickers (previously Wilson Road), Bristol, Wilmott and Avro were all early aircraft companies.

Many of the parishioners of Eastwood are gone, leaving only a name in the roll of honour in the church.

Before the demolition of the cottages in Eastwoodbury Lane, there was a hump-backed bridge outside Cockethurst Farm over the stream. There was also a large pond on the north side of the Lane by the water meadow. Further west, the road dipped down and then ran between high banks for about fifty yards. All these quirks were straightened out when the green belt land to the north of the lane was due to be built on in the 1960's and 1970's.

Jack Porter remembered that there were lots of springs in this area as well as ponds. Legend has it that one of the ponds was so deep that a horse once bolted with a small cart and was drowned there.

The little thatched cottages, Pillar Box and Tea Tree are all gone because they didn't conform to modern building specifications. The workhouse is gone, that stood where the football club ground is today; it had an upper storey projecting and was still being lived in during the 1950's by Sheila Currie and her family; this house belonged to the Fowler Family. In the past, parishes were responsible for the poor in their area. The parish Poor Law, begun in the reign of Elizabeth I, continued through to the middle of the 18th Century; it was implemented in a bid to look after the poor, young and old, able or infirm.

At the start of Rayleigh Road there is at the time of writing a large Ford car showroom. The junction is known as Kent Elms Corner, possibly a corruption of cant elms, meaning leaning elms. The prevailing wind direction could easily have caused this phenomenon. Today all the elms themselves are gone, victim to the march of progress and road-widening schemes as much as to Dutch Elm disease. Before the showroom was here, there was a set of small shops, on either side of the road, including a fishmonger, a cycle shop, a fruiterer, a wine merchant, a general stores and a sweet shop.

Mr and Mrs Bird donated a huge number of photographs to the Eastwood Project, not least being one of the Prince Avenue Pest House, a place for isolating patients in the days before the NHS and modern medicine. The Health Centre and Library at Kent Elms was formally opened on the 13th July, 1964, by the Mayor of Southend, Alderman Morris, J.P. Prior to the opening, a branch library was available every Tuesday at the Eastwood Memorial Hall. There had also been a Brown's Library at Jones' Corner in the 1950's prior to this.

The parade on the other side of the car park has changed hands many times over the years, but at the time of the introduction of the Health Centre, there was Dorkings the sweet shop, Majors the Chemists, the Co-operative grocers, Kent Elms Fisheries, the Daintywear Drapers and The Carlton Bakery.

There have been all kinds of recreational clubs in Eastwood within living memory; these would include the billiards club, the tennis club in Snakes Lane, the Drama Group, the Badminton Club, the Cycling Club, the Craft Club, the Eastwood Ramblers and the Wine Circle. There are still four public houses in Eastwood, although their livelihood is being threatened due to the smoking ban and the drink-driving laws. Mr Fowler left a stipulation in his will that no licensed premises should ever be built on any part of the land that he might sell off for other purposes!

Eastwood seems now to be a suburb of Southend. Its various postcodes place parts of the area in Westcliff, parts in Southend and parts in Leigh. A properly conducted archaeological survey of the few open areas that are left would no doubt reveal much of the Eastwood that has been consumed by its larger neighbour, and it is to be hoped that our early 21st-Century book will one day instigate this to help to paint a fuller picture.

The 1928 census gives evidence and strength to the importance of the existence of agriculture and horticulture, brick making and tile making in the 3000 acres of Eastwood Parish. Today's Eastwood is in a different place and bears little resemblance to the Eastwood remembered by those who have contributed to this book. The final stroke for Old Eastwood was the closure of the Lane that ran through the Parish; Eastwoodbury Lane, named for the Church and for the Bury Priory, was closed to accommodate the expansion of the airport in 2011, splitting an ancient community in half, and destroying the continuity of centuries.

The last field still being ploughed in Eastwood, next to the extended runway.